ETHNOGRAPHY IN ORGANIZATIONS

HELEN B. SCHWARTZMAN
Northwestern University

Qualitative Research Methods
Volume 27

SAGE Publications
International Educational and Professional Publisher
Newbury Park   London   New Delhi

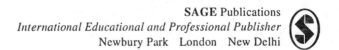

Previous Page: Aerial Photograph of the Hawthorne Works, circa 1945

For information address:

SAGE Publications, Inc.
2455 Teller Road
Newbury Park, California 91320

SAGE Publications Ltd.
6 Bonhill Street
London EC2A 4PU
United Kingdom

SAGE Publications India Pvt. Ltd.
M-32 Market
Greater Kailash I
New Delhi 110 048 India

Printed in the United States of America

Library of Congress Cataloging-in-Publication Data

Schwartzman, Helen B.
    Ethnography in organizations / Helen B. Schwartzman
        p. cm. —(Qualitative research methods ; v. 27)
    Includes bibliographical references.
    ISBN 0-8039-4378-4. — ISBN 0-8039-4379-2 (pbk)
    1. Organizational behavior. 2. Corporate culture. 3. Ethnology—
Methodology. 4. Business anthropology. I. Title. II. Series.
HD58.7.S349 1993
302.3'5—dc20   92-33023
                                                         CIP

93 94 95 96 10 9 8 7 6 5 4 3 2

Sage Production Editor: Judith L. Hunter

CONTENTS

ACKNOWLEDGMENTS

For permisssion to reprint copyrighted material the author and publisher gratefully acknowledge the following:

Photograph of the Hawthorne Works, circa 1945, reproduced courtesy of AT&T Archives.

Photograph of the demolition of Building 27 of the Hawthorne Works, reproduced courtesy of the *Chicago Sun-Times.*

Gregory, K. L., Native-View Paradigms: Multiple Cultures & Culture Conflict in Organizations, *Administrative Science Quarterly*, Volume 28, Number 3, 1983, p. 368, figure 1. Reprinted by permission of *Administrative Science Quarterly.*

Roethlisberger, F. J., & Dickson, W. J., *Management and The Worker,* Cambridge, MA: Harvard University Press, pp. 182-189, 389, 418, 566, & figure 33. Copyright © 1939, 1967 by the President & Fellows of Harvard College. Reprinted by permission of the publisher.

Schwartzman, H. B., The Ethnographic Evaluation of Human Service Programs: Guidelines and an Illustration, *Anthropological Quarterly,* Volume 53, Number 4, 1983, p. 183, figure 1. Reprinted by permission of *Anthropological Quarterly.*

Schwartzman, H. B., *The Meeting: Gatherings in Organizations & Communities*, 1989. New York: Plenum Publishing Corporation, pp. 67-69. Reprinted by permission of Plenum Publishing Corporation.

To the memory of my grandfather
Russell P. Beale
Western Electric Employee for 42 Years
Southern California Installation Department

EDITORS' INTRODUCTION

One among many ways to classify the study of social life is by the kinds of settings in which such study takes place. Villages, societies (large and small), families, urban neighborhoods, hospitals, taverns, factories, governmental agencies, schools, prisons, research laboratories, courtrooms, and so forth all provide sites (and topics) for social study. All have their own rhythms and rules, their own performance standards, and their own troublesome duties for members to carry out that both ease and complicate social research. Increasingly, ethnographers find themselves within private and public work organizations in their own society, attempting to make sense out of whatever cultural uniqueness or consciousness-of-kind such settings provide. These organizations are "formal" in the sense of having explicit tasks to accomplish and "informal" in the sense of the way members continually negotiate with one another in the interpretation and carrying out of such tasks. The promise of ethnography is the presentation of the work culture that emerges from the interplay between these so-called formal and informal aspects of organizational life. While the ethnographic study of work organizations is hardly new, the number of such studies has grown rather dramatically in recent years. Indeed, for better or worse, the phrase *corporate culture* is now a part of our everyday discourse the world over.

Some of the reasons for the renewed interest in the cultural contours of organizations are covered by Helen Schwartzman in the 27th Volume of the Sage Qualitative Research Methods Series. Her intention is to provide readers with some sound advice as to how they might conduct fieldwork in organizations and, in the process, come to an understanding of a work culture as situated in particular places, by particular people, at particular times. Such advice derives both from the author's wide-ranging research experience in several organizational settings and from her sharply focused historical review of the anthropology of work and organization. As such, the monograph moves from the creation myths embodied in the foundational Hawthorne Studies, begun in the late 1920s, to the focused appreciation of daily routines, such as meetings, corridor talk, and paperwork, found in contemporary accounts of organizational cultures. Showing how the past informs the present, or at least should inform the present, is very much at the heart of this monograph.

—John Van Maanen
Peter K. Manning
Marc L. Miller

PREFACE

For the past 18 years I have conducted research, for one reason or another, in a variety of organizational settings in American society. My reasons for conducting this research were not always to study "the organization," but in each project I feel that I learned something new about specific organizations and more general processes of "organizing" (Weick, 1979). My research interests have led me to examine the topic of children's play in a day-care center, a community mental health center in a "psychiatric ghetto," mental health treatment facilities for children in the State of Illinois, the development and transformation of the Hawthorne plant in Chicago and Cicero, and a highly profitable food technology company in the suburbs of Chicago.

In this book I will draw on my experiences working in these various contexts, as well as a historical survey of the anthropological literature, to offer some suggestions for conducting ethnography in organizations. As more and more anthropologists turn their attention to this area of research in American society, it seems important for us to know what past researchers have done as well as to begin sharing research experiences with each other. I would like to thank the editors of Sage's Qualitative Research Methods series—John Van Maanen, Peter K. Manning, and Marc L. Miller—and Mitch Allen for their patience in waiting (a very long time) for this manuscript, for their comments and criticism, and for providing me with the opportunity to reflect on and share my research experiences with readers of this series.

ETHNOGRAPHY IN ORGANIZATIONS

HELEN B. SCHWARTZMAN
Northwestern University

1. INTRODUCTION

Ethnography is the trademark of cultural anthropology. As a method for grasping "the native's point of view" (Malinowski, 1922, p. 25) it was developed by researchers working mostly outside the United States—in Samoa, Kenya, Bali, Brazil. In the 1930s and 1940s, however, ethnographers were also working within the United States, developing innovative ways to use fieldwork techniques in some of the earliest behavioral science investigations of organizations and industries. In this book I present a methodological history of this anthropological research tradition, beginning with the well-known but controversial Hawthorne Studies and continuing into the present. My reason for presenting this discussion of ethnography in organizations this way is because I believe that it is necessary to ground the process and products of organizational ethnography in both the past and the present. In this way researchers who wish to use ethnography for the study of organizations can begin to learn about and appreciate the ways that this method has developed and can begin to make decisions about when and where to employ this approach in their own research.

2

Anthropology and Organizational Research

George Marcus and Michael Fischer suggest that anthropologists have promised enlightenment in two ways: (a) "to salvage distinct cultural forms of life from a process of apparent global Westernization," and (b) "to serve as a form of cultural critique for ourselves. . . . [to] use portraits of other cultural patterns to reflect self-critically on our own ways. . . "(1986, p. 1). Marcus and Fischer conclude that anthropologists have been much better at making good on the first promise, as opposed to the second, but I believe that there is growing evidence that recent research in American society, and particularly on organizations and institutions in the United States, will allow the discipline to finally fulfill this second promise.

Anthropologists have been at the outskirts of research on American organizations for some time; however, recently ethnographers have begun to step back into this field. In fact, this is the discipline's second foray into this area, because anthropologists played an important, although now largely forgotten, role in the Hawthorne study of the 1920s and 1930s and the subsequent human relations movement. It was this research conducted at the Western Electric Hawthorne Plant in western Chicago and Cicero that legitimated the organization behavior research field, but by the 1950s anthropologists had largely abandoned this area to other researchers. Today, however, anthropologists are returning to the study of complex organizations, and so the tradition of industrial ethnology is rejuvenating itself as the anthropology of work, and ethnographers are studying public bureaucracies and investigating the culture of corporations and occupations (e.g., Briody & Baba, 1991; Britan & Cohen, 1980; Dubinskas, 1988; Gamst, 1980; Gregory, 1983; Nash, 1989; Safa, 1986; Schwartzman, 1989; Van Maanen, 1982).

These studies have been encouraged by a growing recognition among anthropologists that all societies, no matter how remote, are affected by the actions taken by governmental as well as private organizations. These studies have also been encouraged by the recognition that in American society, as Dan Rose suggests, "It is the corporate form that encases us in our daily life," but it is a form that remains invisible to us (1989, pp. 6, 12). Although it has taken the discipline some time to "bring anthropology back home," anthropologists are well situated to examine the processes of organizational life and incorporation that have become so familiar to us that we do not seem to see them. More and more researchers both within and outside the discipline of anthropology have begun to recognize that ethnography is a particularly valuable method of research because it problematicizes the ways that individuals and groups constitute and interpret organizations and societies on a daily interactional basis.

Hawthorne and the History of Organizational Research

In this book the Hawthorne study is analyzed in detail both because of the impact that it had on subsequent research on organizations and because the controversies and critiques that it generated provide us with an interesting perspective on the range of roles and methods that organizational ethnographers may use. The social, political, and economic changes that characterize the history of American society between 1927 and the present day are reflected in the history of ethnographic research on American organizations that I present here. Initially, research was focused on large industrial organizations, such as the Hawthorne plant, and the practice of industrial ethnology was therefore rooted in the practice of welfare capitalism as it was utilized by large corporations at this time (see Burawoy, 1979). Following the Depression, and with the expansion of the public and service sectors of the economy after World War II, researchers in a variety of fields (especially sociology) began to use fieldwork techniques to study public sector bureaucracies, such as the TVA and other federal and state agencies. The social and political movements of the 1960s spawned some interest in the study of alternative and antibureaucratic organizations, but it was not until the 1970s and 1980s that researchers within the discipline of anthropology began to turn their attention once again to the study of formal organizations and the place of work in American society. In the 1980s and 1990s researchers have used ethnographic methods to examine a variety of organizations in the United States, including studies of traditional industries, such as railroads, as well as more recent high-tech industries, occupations, and communities, such as computer professionals in Silicon Valley.

The Field and Fieldwork: Cultures From the Inside Out

One of the defining characteristics of ethnographic research is that the investigator goes into the field, instead of bringing the field to the investigator. Ethnographers go into the field to learn about a culture from the inside out. In this book I discuss the various ways that researchers have developed for learning about the cultures and structures of organizations from the inside out. Ethnography facilitates this learning process in several ways. First, it provides researchers with a way to examine the cultural knowledge, behavior, and artifacts that participants share and use to interpret their experiences in a group (Spradley, 1980, pp. 10, 30, 31). In conjunction with this, ethnography also requires researchers to examine the taken for granted, but very important, ideas and practices that influence the way lives are lived, and constructed, in organizational contexts. Because ethnographers are directed to examine both what people say and what people do, it is possible to understand the way that everyday routines constitute and reconstitute organizational and societal structures. Researchers from a number of different theoretical traditions have begun to recognize the value of linking these micro-level, interactional processes with macro-level structures, and ethnography provides researchers with the kind of data necessary to make this link.

Organization of the Book

To present both a methodological history of ethnography in organizations and methodological guidelines for the conduct of ethnography in organizations, this book is organized in the following manner. In Chapter 2 the Hawthorne study is described in detail, and managerial interpretations as well as theoretical and methodological implications are examined. In Chapter 3 I discuss the role that anthropologists played in the human relation studies that developed as a outgrowth of the Hawthorne research. The disappearance of anthropologists from the field of organizational research is also considered here. In Chapter 4 recent studies of work and organizations are described, including recent research in the anthropology of work, studies of occupational and organizational culture, and the study of organizing processes in organizations. In Chapter 5 I present some guidelines for the conduct of ethnography in organizations, using the experiences of researchers discussed in the previous chapters and drawing on my own experiences studying organizations for the past 18 years. Chapter 6 offers a brief postscript on the Hawthorne study and the Hawthorne plant.

2. WHAT HAPPENED AT HAWTHORNE?

The Hawthorne researches started out as "hypothesis testing" and in time became more "hypothesis generating" studies. As in terms of conventional procedures this progression looks like going backwards, we have tried to provide a logic for why it went this way.

William Dickson and
Fritz J. Roethlisberger
(1966, p. 46)

The most influential behavioral science study of a business enterprise is still, even after 50 years, the Hawthorne study—reported originally by F. J. Roethlisberger and William Dickson in *Management and the Worker* (1939).[1] The Hawthorne research is one of the creation myths of industrial psychologists and sociologists, as noted by Bramel and Friend (1981). The study began as a test of the scientific management principles associated with the work of Frederick W. Taylor (1947), but it took a surprising turn and ended by disqualifying the major principles on which scientific management was based. In the process, the informal organization of workers was discovered, and a new research tradition, the human relations school, was born. The role that anthropologists, and especially anthropological methods and theories, played in this early work on American organizations has only recently been rediscovered by researchers within, as well as outside of, the discipline.

The Hawthorne Studies

The Hawthorne plant, which was the subject of the study, was located partly in western Chicago and partly in the town of Cicero, Illinois, and served as one of the major supply organizations for the Western Electric Company (itself a division of the Bell Telephone System). In 1927, when the project began, there were 29,000 employees at the Hawthorne Works, representing more than 60 nationalities (Roethlisberger & Dickson, 1939, p. 6). The study was initiated because Western Electric management was interested in understanding relationships between fatigue and monotony and job satisfaction and dissatisfaction. A series of experiments conducted by the company, beginning in 1924, had specifically attempted to examine relationships between illumination intensity and productivity. However, the results of these investigations were confusing and difficult to interpret. "Some of the results of this experiment seemed to say that it [the relationship of illumination to productivity] was positive, some that it was zero, and some that it was screwy" (Dickson & Roethlisberger, 1966, p. 20). In some cases, increase in illumination was accompanied by an increase in output, but sometimes this produced no increase, and the "screwy" part was that frequently when the illumination intensity was decreased, output remained the same or even went up. In one instance, illumination was reduced to an intensity approximating moonlight, and two operators continued producing at their improved rate (Roethlisberger & Dickson, 1939, p. 17).

THE EXPERIMENTS

A series of tests, which came to be known as the Relay Assembly Test Room (RATR) experiments and the Mica Splitting Test Room experiments, were designed to examine this issue in more detail. A specific attempt was made here to approximate conditions in a controlled experiment. In the case of the first RATR experiment (the most famous of these investigations) five female operators, involved in the assembly of small electrical relays for telephones, were segregated in a room. Baseline data on the operators output were first collected, and then the effect of a variety of experimental changes (e.g., rest pauses, shorter working days, free lunches, small-group incentive payment plans) on productivity was examined over a span of 24 experimental periods. It was during this phase of the study that Western Electric personnel turned to the Harvard Business School for consultation about the project, and especially its puzzling findings. Elton Mayo, a psychologist, became involved with the study at this point and he in turn involved Fritz J. Roethlisberger, who began to work with William Dickson and several other researchers within the company on examining the results of these experiments.

The most interesting and controversial finding reported from this early phase of the study (illumination, and especially the RATR experiments) has come to be known as the Hawthorne Effect: the "unexpected impact of nonexperimental variables on experimental outcomes" (Finlay, 1991, p. 1820). In the later experiments the researchers were once again puzzled by the fact that a general improvement in output for the operators was noted, but it rose independently of the specific changes in working conditions that were introduced, and it also rose when the rewards were withdrawn. (This finding has been repeatedly challenged in reinterpretations of the Hawthorne research; e.g., see Bramel & Friend, 1981). The operators were also puzzled by these findings, as they reported no sensation of working faster, but they thought that it might have something to do with the absence of supervision they experienced in the room (in this case, the investigators had basically taken over the role of supervisors). The investigators began to note that the study itself might be contributing to the puzzling results. And it was also suggested that just attempting to listen sympathetically to workers, as well as the status and attention associated with being studied, might be factors contributing to the continued increase in productivity. This interpretation of results had a great impact on the future course of the study:

> It is apparent that the logic of a controlled experiment was responsible for many strange occurrences in the test room. It prompted the experimenters on one occasion to transfer two operators back to the department and substitute two other operators. It caused them to interview girls in the superintendent's office and otherwise to extend to them privileges hitherto unheard of in the ordinary shop department. In the endeavor to keep the major variables in the situation constant and the girls' attitudes co-operative, the investigators inadvertently altered the total social situation of the group. . . . In the process of setting the conditions for the test, they had altered completely the social situation of the operators and their customary attitudes and interpersonal relations.
>
> With this realization, the inquiry changed its character. No longer were the investigators interested in testing for the effects of single variables. In the place of a controlled experiment, they substituted the notion of a social system which needed to be described and understood as a system of interdependent elements. This situation included not only the external events but the meanings which individuals assigned to them: their attitudes toward them and their preoccupations about them. Rather than trying to keep these "psychological factors" constant, the investigators had to regard them as important variables in the situation. As much attention had to be given to these psychological factors as to output in assessing the external changes which took place. (Roethlisberger & Dickson, 1939, pp. 182-184).

THE INTERVIEWS

To explore the nature of these "psychological factors," as well as possibilities for improving supervision, the investigators shifted their methodological approach and initiated a large-scale interview study, involving more than 30 interviewers and more than 20,000 workers, conducted between September 1928 and early 1931. It was noted that the nondirective interview style that was developed had a very cathartic effect on workers.[2] The focus of these interviews became those matters of interest and concern to employees, and here the investigators observed a shared concern among individuals to remain in specific work groups, sometimes even when a switch in job would mean higher pay. For example, in one interview:

> A girl of eighteen protested to the interviewer that her mother was continually urging her to ask Mr. X, her supervisor, for a "raise." She had refused, but her loyalty to her mother and the pressure the latter exerted were affecting her work and her relations at work. She talked her situation out with an interviewer, and it became clear that to her a "raise" would mean departure from her daily companions and associates. (Mayo, 1949, p. 73)

The interviews also revealed a uniformity of behavior (or banding together) of certain groups, often for the purpose of protection against practices that were interpreted as menacing to the groups' welfare. This gradually came to be conceptualized as the social system or social organization of the group. The investigators decided to examine the development and nature of such groups more extensively, which led to another methodological switch and to the creation of the Bank Wiring Observation Room. Observations were conducted here between November 1931 and May 1932, during the height of the Depression in the United States.

THE OBSERVATIONS

This study was designed as a "direct observation study" that would focus on the overt behavior of a group of 14 male operators working in a shop department on the task of connecting bands of terminals with color-coded wires (see Figure 2.1). This group was placed in a separate observation/work room in order to facilitate observations and record keeping. In this case the researchers were specifically interested in supplementing interviews with direct observations that would inform them about not only what workers *said* they did but what they actually *did* in a work context (Roethlisberger & Dickson, 1939, p. 385). In designing this new method, Roethlisberger and Dickson were influenced by the anthropologist W. Lloyd Warner, who suggested that the work group could be examined as a type of small society, and as such was amenable to the observational techniques of fieldwork. Warner (a student of Radcliffe-Brown, Malinowski, and Lowie) had recently returned from conducting fieldwork among the Murngin in Australia, but he was very interested in developing ways to use anthropology for the study of modern societies. Mayo was particularly receptive to these suggestions because he was a friend of both Malinowski and Radcliffe-Brown. Roethlisberger and Dickson note a particular debt to Warner in *Management and the Worker* (1939):

> The general methodological concepts employed throughout this study [the Bank Wiring Observation Room] were chiefly derived from Mr. Warner; however, he should not in any sense be held responsible for their detailed application to this industrial situation. Mr. Warner frequently discussed the investigators' problems with them and called their attention to the similarities between the problems confronting them and those confronting the anthropological field worker, He also directed their attention to the works of such people as Durkheim, Malinowski, Radcliffe-Brown, and Georg Simmel, from which a wealth of background material was obtained. (p. 389)

As discussed most explicitly in the chapter, "Method and Procedure in a Shop Department," this approach focused on the collection of detailed information on the workers and their relationships to each other (behavioral observations) and also on the meaning of their work (e.g., what constitutes a day's work) and their activities in this context (interview information). The research work itself was conducted by two different investigators: (a) an observer who was placed within the group in the role of "disinterested spectator" and who was expected to keep records of work performance as well as records of significant events, conversations, and interactions; and (b) an interviewer who acted as an outsider to the group and did not go into the observation room but remained in contact with the observer and conducted interviews specifically designed "to gain some insight into [worker] attitudes, thoughts and feelings" (Roethlisberger and Dickson, 1939, pp. 388, 391). For the first time in organizational research this new method produced "a systematic description of the social organization of an industrial working group" (Chapple, 1953, p. 820).

Figure 2.1. Bank Wiring Observation Room

SOURCE: Reprinted by permission from *Management and the Worker* by F. J. Roethlisberger and William J. Dickson, Cambridge, MA: Harvard University Press, Copyright © 1939, 1967 by the President and Fellows of Harvard College.

10

It was during the Bank Wiring Observarion Room (BWOR) stage of this study that the influence of workers' informal organization on productivity was discovered. In the observation context, the effect of group pressure and group beliefs on the group's total output of terminal units was specifically noted. In this case, the informal organization worked against the wage incentive system that management had recently introduced to increase productivity.

Workers in the BWOR were operating under a complicated system of group piecework, in which "the entire department was considered a unit for purposes of payment" (Roethlisberger & Dickson, 1939, p. 409). In this case each worker received, in addition to a guaranteed hourly wage, a sum based on the amount by which the production of the department as a whole exceeded the total guaranteed hourly rate earnings of its members. The department was credited with a fixed sum for every unit produced. This system was based on the assumption that all employees would attempt to increase, or at least maintain, their total group output. Management believed that a day's work would be determined at the point where fatigue and/or pain costs were balanced by the estimate of added monetary return. This was expected to lead the group to exert pressure on slower workers, but the observations and interviews conducted in the BWOR revealed that the opposite occurred.

In this setting, a day's work came to be defined as a specified number of units to be completed each day by each worker. The standard the group agreed on was considerably lower than what management had anticipated, so it could not function as a competitive standard. Any individual whose work exceeded this standard was looked upon with disfavor and negatively labelled "slave," "speed king," "runt," and "rate-buster," and a number of sanctions were developed to bring people in line ("binging," sarcasm, ostracism). In other words, instead of exerting pressure on slower workers, the group's informal organization led to pressure being placed upon faster workers, the so-called "rate-busters." An interchange between two workers, reported by Roethlisberger and Dickson, reveals this pattern. In this case, W6 was one of the faster wiremen in the group, whereas W8 was one of the slower ones:

W8 (to W6): "Why don't you quit work? Let's see, this is your thirty-fifth row today. What are you going to do with them all?"

W6: "What do you care? It's to your advantage if I work, isn't it?"

W8: "Yeah, but the way you're working you'll get stuck with them" (meaning that W6 would have to refrain from reporting all the work he did)

W6: "Don't worry about that. I'll take care of it. You're getting paid by the sets I turn out. That's all you should worry about."

W8: "If you don't quit work I'll bing you." W8 struck W6 and finally chased him around the room.

Observer (a few minutes later): "What's the matter, W6, won't he let you work?"

W6: "No. I'm all through though. I've got enough done." W6 then went over and helped another wireman. This practice was sanctioned by the group. (Roethlisberger & Dickson, 1934, p. 9)

Supporting the rate-buster phenomenon was the group's belief that if they increased their output, either the standard would be raised, the hourly rate would be cut, or someone would be laid off. This belief is expressed in an interview with another wireman from the BWOR.

Interviewer: "You say there is no incentive to turn out more work. If all of you did more work, wouldn't you make more money?"

W4: "No we wouldn't. They told us that down there one time. You know, the supervisors came around and told us that very thing, that if we would turn out more work we would make more money, but we can't see it that way. Probably what would happen is that our bogey [standard] would be raised, and then we would just be turning out more work for the same money. I can't see that." (Roethlisberger & Dickson, 1939, p. 418)[3]

Interpreting the Results

MANAGERIAL INTERPRETATIONS

The results of the Hawthorne research were used by Roethlisberger and Dickson, and especially Elton Mayo, to illustrate the contradiction between formal and informal organization evident in all industrial plants. *Formal organization* was understood here to "refer to those patterns of interaction prescribed by the rules and regulations of the company as well as to the policies which prescribe the relations that obtain . . . within the human organization (individuals and groups) and the technical (logical deployment of materials, tools, machines, and products) organization." In contrast, *informal organization* referred "to the actual personal interrelations existing among the members of the organization which are not represented by . . . the formal organization" (Roethlisberger & Dickson, 1939, p. 566).

The researchers used this distinction between formal and informal organization to suggest that management may have been mistaken to assume that workers were necessarily motivated only by economic, or "rational," interests, as the wage incentive system assumed. In interpreting the results of research conducted in both the RATR and the BWOR, the researchers argued that the informal organization could work either for or against "the economic objectives of the enterprise" (Roethlisberger & Dickson, 1939, p. xiii) and that workers were motivated as much by a "logic of sentiments" as by a "logic of efficiency" (pp. 566-567). In the case of the RATR the power of the informal organization worked for these objectives by increasing production, but in the case of the BWOR the informal organization worked against these objectives by restricting and stabilizing production. Bramel and Friend suggest that Mayo was especially impressed with this contrast and that his "persistent advocacy of 'human relations in industry' found its rationale in the problem of how to manipulate workers in such a way as to harness the power of the cohesive group in the 'good' direction [relay assembly] rather than have that power turned against management [bank wiring]" (Bramel & Friend, 1981, p. 874).

The major managerial innovation produced by Hawthorne was the development of what came to be known as the counseling program. The Hawthorne researchers appeared to have been most impressed by the non-directive interview approach and they concluded that the installation of such a program on a permanent basis would be of major therapeutic value to the organization and individuals in the organization (Chapple, 1953, p. 821). Counseling programs based on this approach became widespread within the AT&T system as well as other organizations (see Dickson & Roethlisberger, 1966). The multiple roles of observer, researcher, diagnostician, listener, helper and communicator, outlined by Dickson and Roethlisberger, illustrate how the counseling program was conceptualized and became instituted and perceived as a valuable personnel tool for management (1966, pp. 40-41).

Over the years the Hawthorne study has been subjected to increasing criticism of its management bias and paternalistic orientation (e.g., Clegg & Dunkerly, 1980). While recognizing that the study was significant because it challenged Taylor's (1947) "economic man" and replaced this image with workers who were seen as having both social and psychological needs and interests, the validity of these interpretations has been questioned by many researchers (see an early review of human relations research by Wilensky, 1957). For example, the study has been specifically criticized for portraying workers as illogical and irrational (e.g., the restriction of output in the BWOR) when, in fact, these actions may have been very rational, especially given the historical context of the research (Bramel & Friend, 1981; Clegg & Dunkerly, 1980).[4] Elton Mayo, and his "popularizing tendencies," are generally singled out in these evaluations. For example, Rose (1975) attacks the spread of "Mayoism" following the Hawthorne research:

> Mayoism emerged rapidly as the twentieth century's most seductive managerial ideology. What, after all, could be more appealing than to be told that one's subordinates are non-logical; that their uncooperativeness is a frustrated urge to collaborate; that their demands for cash mark a need for your approval; and that you have a historic destiny as a broker of social harmony? (p. 124)

Subsequent studies by researchers such as Roy (1954) illustrated how machine operators, in order to make their work rates, had to form informal groups and practices to counter the inefficiency and illogic of managerial regulations, which obstructed the work and output of operators. Here the workers behaved "rationally" in an attempt to counter the "irrationality" of management.

THEORETICAL IMPLICATIONS

While managers and researchers have drawn many different conclusions about the significance of the Hawthorne research, Burrell and Morgan (1979) argue that the most significant effect of this study is theoretical. In their view the Hawthorne study represents an important landmark in the introduction of systems equilibrium concepts and an organic metaphor (as taken from the work of Durkheim, Malinowski, and especially Pareto and Radcliffe-Brown)[5] into the organizational literature (see Burrell & Morgan, 1979, p. 132; also pp. 130-143). The influence of functionalist researchers, including anthropologists, is particularly evident in Roethlisberger and Dickson's (1939) discussion of their view of an industrial organization:

> The point of view which gradually emerged from these studies is one from which an industrial organization is regarded as a social system. . . . By "system" is meant something which must be considered as a whole

15

because each part bears a relation of interdependence to every other part (p. 551). . . . Any changes in one part of the social system are accompanied by changes in other parts of the system. The parts of the system can be conceived of as being in a state of equilibrium. (p. 567)

In the 1990s the problems of systems, equilibrium, and homeostatic models are well known; however, while recognizing the drawbacks of these models, Burrell and Morgan (1979, pp. 142-143) suggest that the Hawthorne research remains significant because it "marked a clear advance over the simple factor explanations offered by the classical management theorists and industrial psychologists" and that it also anticipated a number of other theoretical developments, such as socio-technical systems theory (e.g., Trist & Bamforth, 1951) and the action frame of reference (e.g., Silverman, 1970).

METHODOLOGICAL IMPLICATIONS

The current methodological reading of Hawthorne is quite negative. Over the years the study has been scrutinized by many researchers and subjected to multiple analyses and reanalyses. In particular the RATR data have been analyzed and a variety of problems have been found with the data collection techniques, experimental design, and actual results as well as the investigators' interpretation of results (e.g., Carey, 1967; Franke & Kaul, 1978; Landsberger, 1958). The barrage of criticism has been so thorough, detailed, and constant that Burrell and Morgan suggest that "in many quarters the [Hawthorne Studies] are now largely discredited as a piece of social research" (1979, p. 130). It is for this reason that Burrell and Morgan argue that the most important contribution of Hawthorne today is theoretical rather than empirical. In my view, however, there is an important methodological message in this study.

The methodological message of Hawthorne has been difficult to hear because of the barrage of criticism directed toward the specific methods employed in the RATR as well as the interpretation of the data produced by the study. In my view, the most significant contribution of this project is its demonstration of the value of allowing both research questions and methods to evolve and change during the course of an investigation. This is most evident when it is realized that the study evolved from a controlled experiment (the illumination and Relay Assembly Test Room experiments), to an interview study, and finally to a qualitative/fieldwork investigation (the Bank Wiring Observation Room). What is significant here is that as the researchers developed new questions, they allowed themselves the luxury of using or developing not only new methods (rather than attempting only to tighten or fix their initial method) but also new questions. William Dickson presents a summary of some of the choices made by the researchers in this regard. Here he is discussing the investigators' response to results from the initial illumination experiments, the results from the Relay Assembly Test Room and the so-called Hawthorne Effect, and the interview phases of the project:

1. When the Hawthorne effect produced both (a) inconclusive experimental results and (b) a peculiar positive result, the Hawthorne investigators could have gone down path (a) and tried to improve their experimental designs. Instead they chose to go down path (b) on a chase for the positive effect. This involved them in a more clinical and situational approach.
2. When they started interviewing workers and saw that they could get their data from both (a) answers by workers to their direct questions or (b) behaving in a way which would help the workers to say what was important to them, they could have gone down path (a) and tried to improve their questionnaire designs and sampling techniques. Instead they went down (b) and tried to develop clinically their interviewing skills. . . .

The Hawthorne researches started out as "hypothesis testing" and in time became more "hypothesis generating" studies. As in terms of conventional procedures this progression looks like going backwards, we have tried to provide a logic for why it went this way. (Dickson & Roethlisberger, 1966, p. 46)

It is very likely that if the above choices had not been made, then the Hawthorne study would not be the pioneering investigation it is generally thought to be, even given the criticism and refutation of specific results. It is also true that if the researchers had not chosen to go "backwards," then they would not have produced a study that W. F. Whyte suggests is still, even after 50 years, "unsurpassed for detailed, systematic observational records of the behavior of work groups" (1978, p. 418). One point frequently missed in the critiques of Hawthorne is that it is the richness of the original research data itself that has provided investigators with material to formulate reinterpretations of the study (Whyte, 1978, p. 418).

Summary: The Methodological Message of Hawthorne

When looked at in this fashion, the Hawthorne investigation presents a strong argument for the use of ethnographic and qualitative methods in the study of organizations. Most organizational researchers (with some notable exceptions), however, have drawn the opposite lesson from this research and have returned to the use of experimental/quantitative methods (especially evident in industrial/organizational psychology) or interview/survey methods (associated with organizational sociology). The Hawthorne researchers themselves settled on the interview technique and the counselor role as the major research and personnel tools to develop (see Dickson & Roethlisberger, 1966), thereby neglecting the development of observational and situational techniques for understanding organizations and organizational behavior (Chapple, 1953).[6] It was left to a group of human relations researchers, who were both anthropologists and sociologists, to further develop what I have interpreted here as the methodological message of Hawthorne. This research tradition will be examined in Chapter 3.

NOTES

1. I take the title of this chapter from a 1974 article by H. M. Parsons, titled "What Happened at Hawthorne?" in which he reinterprets the results of this research project by suggesting that the controversial Hawthorne Effect was the result of operant reinforcement contingencies, that is, the Relay Assembly Test Room operators "were told what their output rates were, and the higher the rates, the more money they earned" (p. 922). Therefore, Parsons suggests that a "variable that had remained in obscurity emerges: the consequences of responding. The variable consisted of information feedback coupled with financial reward" (p. 922).

2. This interviewing approach was apparently developed independently of Carl Rogers' client-centered therapy techniques, although there are many interesting parallels between the two approaches (Chapple, 1953, p. 821). For a complete description of the interviewing method employed, see Roethlisberger and Dickson (1939, pp. 270-291); and for a discussion of the counseling program that developed out of this phase of the study, see Dickson and Roethlisberger (1966).

3. According to Roethlisberger and Dickson (1939, pp. 410, 418), raising the bogey could not have had this effect unless it resulted in lower output. However, quite common among the workers was the suspicion that increased output would result in changes in piece rate, so that pay gains would soon be lost while work rates were increased (Bramel & Friend, 1981).

4. According to one of the most recent books on Hawthorne, *Manufacturing Knowledge* (Gillespie, 1991), William Dickson argued in "one of his early reports that [work

18

restriction in the BWOR] was a form of both resistance to managerial control and economic self-defense," but Mayo's psychological interpretations of personal maladjustment
overrode Dickson's political and economic analysis (Finley, 1991, p. 1821).

5. The influence of Radcliffe-Brown's ethnography, *The Andaman Islanders* (1933),
is specifically noted in the investigators' discussion of supervisors' complaints and social
equilibrium (pp. 358-376). The work of Malinowski (see especially 1927), Pitt-Rivers
(1927) and again Radcliffe-Brown (1933) also influenced the development of the investigators' interview methods (see Roethlisberger & Dickson, 1939, p. 272).

6. When reflecting back on the Hawthorne research, both Eliot Chapple and William
F. Whyte suggest that it was the interview bias of the researchers that retarded the
development of systematic observation and interviewing techniques for organizational
researchers (see Chapple, 1953, p. 821, and Whyte, 1978, p. 414). In Whyte's view the
development of the counseling program "was one of the most monumental misunderstandings of the implication of social research in the course of intellectual history" (p. 414).

3. WHAT HAPPENED TO ANTHROPOLOGY?

*[The] observance of group-sanctioned behavior and attitudes "fills out"
the rationally conceived organization. What is on paper an organization
becomes a "living, breathing" social organism, with all the intricacies,
emotions, and contradictions we associate with human relations. While
no organization would long persist which did not provide its members
with this opportunity for spontaneous "human relations," a major problem of the larger organization becomes one of successfully incorporating
the small group.*

Leonard Sayles (1957, p. 145)

The methodological message of Hawthorne was interpreted by one
group of researchers working in the United States in the 1930s and
1940s. These investigators identified themselves as working within the
human relations school of industrial research and many of them were
anthropologists and sociologists who were at Harvard at the same
time that Mayo, Roethlisberger, and Dickson were working on the
Hawthorne study. Some of the researchers associated with this school
include Conrad Arensberg, Eliot Chapple, Burleigh Gardner, Robert A.
Guest, Solon T. Kimball, F. L. W. Richardson, Leonard Sayles, Charles
R. Walker, W. Lloyd Warner, and William F. Whyte.

The original Hawthorne researchers argued strongly that the project
demonstrated the overriding importance of "human relations factors"
in the workplace (Chapple, 1953, p. 820), but researchers differed in a
variety of ways on how best to study these factors.[1] The anthropologists

and sociologists working within this area developed two general orientations to human relations research: (a) interactional studies associated most specifically with the work of Eliot Chapple, and (b) stratification studies associated with the work of W. Lloyd Warner (see Arensberg, 1951).

Anthropology and Industry: Early Studies

In the first volume of the journal *Applied Anthropology* (later to become *Human Organization*), Chapple presented a critique of the technical/economic interpretation of organization problems, and he used the systems framework (already discussed in Chapter 2) to suggest that an organization can best be studied as a system of relationships between individuals:

> If we look upon organization, therefore, as a system of relations of individuals in which the actual contacts imposed by particular technical processes provide the framework within which people have to reach an equilibrium, it can be seen that the frequency and extent of disturbing situations will determine the kind of teamwork which will result. Thus by making a detailed study of the frequency of these contacts, the degree to which adjustment takes place between the individuals, and the amount of change which takes place as a result of the operation of the organization, we can set up a system of control by which organizations' problems can be dealt with objectively. (1941, p. 6)

Chapple's stress on the interactional and systemic nature of organization was only one aspect of his more general theory of anthropology and human behavior (see Chapple & Coon, 1942). Chapple was specifically interested in developing more systematic ways to record the directly observable activity of individuals in interaction with one another (e.g., time of interaction, pace and tempo, actions reflected through sound and/or the action of skeletal muscles) (Chapple, 1953, p. 827). He was concerned with answering the question "Who does what with whom, when and where?" but he was not concerned with "why" because "you cannot observe *why* anyone does anything" (Whyte, 1984, p. 84). As applied to industrial settings, Chapple (1953) believed that:

> [T]he first task of an investigator in the industrial field is to secure a complete description of the order of actions as they occur spatially within the physical layout of the factory, in flow-chart form, as they involve the

physical processing either of materials or of pieces of paper or whatever requires an action of one person before another person can be in a position to act. (p. 827)

Information about these interactions would be obtained either by direct observation, sometimes using a computing machine, referred to as an "Interaction Chronograph," developed by Chapple for the measurement of interaction (see Chapple, 1949b), or by the use of contact questionnaires (see Chapple, 1949a). In order to change an organization that had developed problems, Chapple believed that it was necessary to change the interactional system and cultural patterns and routines in such settings. In his view it was not enough for individuals and groups to gain insight into the nature and causes of problems, it was also necessary to develop changes in routines and patterns of interaction (see 1953, p. 826).

The work of F. L. W. Richardson is a good example of the application of Chapple's interactional methods to the study of an industrial site. Utilizing Chapple's methods, Richardson and Walker (1948) set out to examine change in employer/employee relationships in a manufacturing plant that at the time was a small but growing business enterprise known as International Business Machines. The Endicott plant of IBM had doubled in size between 1940 and 1947, and the investigators were particularly interested in examining the relation of growth and size to "good human relations" (p. 2). Change in both vertical and horizontal contacts during this time period were specifically considered. It was found that contrary to what might be expected, human relations improved during this growth period because of several changes in organizational structure instituted by the company (e.g., making foremen "personnel managers," abolishing department meetings and instituting "all-company, all level meetings," creating supervisor classes, and so on). What was most important about these changes in plant organization, according to Richardson and Walker, was that "those contacts which drew men together into a satisfactory integration with their fellows *increased*; those which opposed men to one another and tended to weaken integration *decreased*" (p. 91).

W. Lloyd Warner and Yankee City

W. Lloyd Warner's influence on the Hawthorne study has already been examined. It was his specific desire to apply anthropology to the study of contemporary society, even before he began his study of the Murngin in Australia. Somehow, according to Warner, the study of primitive man should shed light on modern man.

When I went to Australia, I told my friends, Professor Robert H. Lowie and Professor Alfred Radcliffe-Brown, that my fundamental purpose in studying primitive man was to know modern man better; that someday I proposed to investigate (just how I did not then know) the social life of modern man with the hope of ultimately placing the research in a larger framework of comparison which would include the other societies of the world. (Warner & Lunt, 1941, p. 3)

Of course, Warner did find a way to study the social life of modern man as he went on to conduct the first large-scale anthropological study of a contemporary community—the now famous Yankee City (Newburyport, Massachusetts) project. Many of the human relations researchers discussed in this chapter, such as Arensberg, Chapple, Gardner, Richardson, and Kimball, worked with Warner on Yankee City in the 1930s. This project examined the social stratification of a community, using anthropological techniques that rejected a priori determinations of social class (such as income, housing, and level of education) and instead focused on the direct observation of social behavior (such as how groups were formed, who interacted with whom) as well as interviews with informants (specifically about what the people of Yankee City felt were the significant groupings among them) (Eddy & Partridge, 1978, p. 18). As with the Hawthorne study, Warner emphasized the importance of combining interviews with observations in order to gain information about these issues. For example if an activity, like a meeting, could be anticipated, researchers would be encouraged "to interview the principal actors both beforehand and afterward" as well to observe the event themselves (Whyte, 1984, p. 92). As field anthropologists working in a contemporary American community, Yankee City researchers were required to be good observers, good reporters (i.e., recorders of observations) and most important, to learn the significance "of detail, meticulous detail, even if he was dealing with the commonplace" (Gardner & Moore, 1964, p. 96).

The influence and importance of the corporation and the voluntary association for understanding American communities were specifically examined in this study. In *The Social System of the Modern Factory*

(1947), Warner and Low extended the Hawthorne research by examining not only the internal dynamics of life in a shoe factory in Yankee City, but also the community context of the factory, and the historical sources of industrial conflict that resulted in a strike. Using this broader analytic framework the investigators were able to relate the strike to changing factory production techniques, labor relations, the increasing mechanization of the production process, and the resulting loss of control experienced by workers. Burawoy (1979) suggests that Warner and Low's study deserves much more attention than it has typically received because, unlike other human relations approaches, this study moves far beyond considering only shop floor conditions to an examination of "the economic, political, and social forces which were transforming relations between capital and labor in the 1930s" (1979, p. 238).

When Warner moved from Harvard to the University of Chicago in 1936, he founded the Committee on Human Relations in Industry with Burleigh Gardner, an anthropologist who had also worked with Warner on the Yankee City project and who also spent 5 years working at the Hawthorne plant helping to implement the interviewing/counseling program (Chapple, 1953, p. 823). This committee initiated and supported a variety of human relations studies, including Gardner's first comprehensive human relations textbook, *Human Relations in Industry*, (Gardner & Moore, 1964), and also W. F. Whyte's study, *Human Relations in the Restaurant Industry* (1948). This investigation of Stouffers restaurants in Chicago is a good example of the use of observations and interviews to examine in detail interactions between participants, work flow, work pressures, and job status. This investigation also illustrates the use of technology to solve what were defined as human relations problems. For example, in the restaurant industry there is a conflict between the social status and the technical requirements of the jobs involved in restaurant operations. Chefs are of higher status than waitresses, and yet the work flow requires waitresses to initiate orders to chefs, thereby leading to conflict between these two groups. In this book Whyte shows how the spindle, a simple technological device for handling orders, could mediate and alleviate face-to-face conflict when it was placed between the chefs and the waitresses.

Although the human relations assumption, that changes in supervisory and group relationships lead to improvement in work efficiency and satisfaction, has been challenged by researchers working both within and outside this tradition (see Wilensky, 1957), this research approach has made many significant contributions to the organizational literature. For example, human relations studies have contributed to our understanding of how workers interact with each other as well as management in specific job situations (Walker & Guest, 1952); how workers accommodate to the monotony of repetitive, unskilled jobs (see especially Roy, 1952, 1959); how workers develop informal relationships that may support and/or resist management goals (see Roy 1952, 1954); how union and management problems are handled on a day-to-day basis (Dalton, 1959); and the interpersonal processes and dynamics of collective bargaining (see Haire, 1957).

Reactions to Anthropologists in Industry, Business, and Bureaucracy

In a 1953 review of applied anthropology in industry, Eliot Chapple summarized the importance and potential of this field for anthropology and industrial researchers. In the early 1950s it still appeared that anthropology would be a significant force in this area, and he wanted to encourage anthropologists to consider the field of industry as a new and rewarding research area:

> [I]t is perhaps worthwhile to stress the potentialities for research by anthropologists in industry. This is particularly true for those persons who are interested in the specific impact of culture through its techniques, processes, and the like on human relations. The individual investigator has available a wide variety of cultural factors and a multiplicity of industrial and business organizations built upon them within the continental limits of the United States. . . . Moreover, in business or industry or government for that matter, on the job in any case, the anthropologist is dealing with a central activity of people, not merely because such a great proportion of the day is devoted to interaction within it, but also because the job provides within it the major sources of stress in our society. And, pleasantly enough, it is susceptible to the traditional skills of the anthropologist as well as his traditional interest—a hard boiled and hard headed description of the culture of a group in the broadest sense, or, if you prefer, of the social organization of an ongoing group. Once the anthropologist gets over his nostalgia for the vanishing primitive, he will find that the industrial situation affords him a magnificent opportunity to improve his understanding of changes in human relations, not merely through observation over a long period of time, but also through the use of deliberate and controlled experiments. (p. 830)

This could have been the charter for the field of industrial ethnology, but unfortunately, for several reasons this did not happen. What did happen is that beginning in the 1940s and continuing into the 1950s, many of the researchers who pioneered the development of fieldwork and ethnographic methods for the study of human relations in organizations began to turn their attention to other fields or other topics. For example, Burleigh Gardner and W. Lloyd Warner founded the consulting firm of Social Research, Inc.; F. L. W. Richardson, William F. Whyte, and Leonard Sayles took positions in business schools: the University of Virginia Graduate School of Business Administration, the New York State School of Industrial and Labor Relations at Cornell University, and the Graduate School of Business at Columbia University, respectively; and Eliot Chapple began a long career as a consultant for both industrial and social service organizations. Conrad Arensberg and Sol Kimball (see 1965) continued their interest in the study of contemporary societies but focused their attention on the community "as the basic unit of analysis and minimal sample" for the study of all societies (Eddy & Partridge, 1978, p. 34).

Along with the pull from other fields that many human relations researchers experienced, there were also forces within anthropology that helped to push many individuals away from the discipline. In the 1950s researchers who conducted fieldwork in the United States, as opposed to abroad, were not viewed as "real anthropologists." Furthermore, many of the anthropologists associated with human relations work began this work with an interest in applying anthropological knowledge and methods to industry and human problems (Chapple, 1953). In fact, many of these researchers were responsible for creating the Society for Applied Anthropology in 1941.[2] This interest in application was problematic to many traditional anthropologists who wished to separate application from pure research (see Eddy & Partridge, 1978). Finally, the anthropological tendency to "study down," as opposed to "up," worked against individuals who chose to work in business and industrial enterprises.

When viewed from this perspective it is probably no accident that the most commonly studied organizations by anthropologists in the 1950s and 1960s were schools (see Ogbu's 1981 review) and some social service settings, such as mental hospitals, (see Caudill, 1958; Devereux, 1949; Salisbury, 1962). As anthropologists turned away from industrial and organizational studies during this time, the field of organizational sociology began to flourish using fieldwork approaches. This research continued the human relations tradition of questioning economic/ rational man by discovering social man in industry and social service settings, but it also expanded and critiqued this tradition as well by focusing, for example, on the dysfunctions and unanticipated consequences of organizations. Robert Merton's work (e.g., 1968) and also the studies of several of his students have now become classics in this area of organizational research: for example, Peter Blau's *The Dynamics of Bureaucracy* (1963); Phillip Selznick's, *TVA and the Grass Roots* (1966); and Alvin Gouldner's *Patterns of Industrial Bureaucracy* (1954a) and *Wildcat Strike* (1954b).

Summary: Human Relations—Methods and Models

The human relations researchers discussed in this chapter are significant because they continued and expanded the theoretical and methodological message of Hawthorne. Theoretically they continued to work within a systems framework, for the most part, stressing the importance of equilibrium:

> While these several concepts of the "informal group" are not identical . . . they do have one common feature. All stress equilibrium, the development of a system of interpersonal relations which stabilizes the work situation (among subordinates and between superior and subordinates), an interconnected series of friendship linkages, work flow relationships, output levels, and status-income relations. The objectives are the maintenance of individual and group stability by insuring a predictability of day-to-day events and effecting a *modus vivendi* as between individual on-the-job needs and the requirements of the formal organization. (Sayles, 1957, p. 141)

As has been pointed out by many researchers, the model of the human relations school is a management model of industrial relations. The focus of these researchers was on understanding the system of relationships that develops, both between workers and between workers and management, in order to control this system and bring it in line with management goals (see critiques of this management perspective by Burawoy, 1979, and Bramel & Friend, 1981). It is the management bias of this school that has led many researchers to neglect and/or disparage

26

this research tradition. While extremely valid as a critique of both the Hawthorne studies and human relations research, this view had made it difficult to assess or even recognize the methodological contributions of human relations studies. It was the human relations tradition that first introduced the term *culture* into the vocabulary of organizational researchers (see Chapple, 1953) by developing ways to combine interviews and observations of interactions in specific work settings, anticipating by several years the organizational culture studies of the 1980s. It was human relations researchers who first tried to study up in anthropology, focusing on industrial settings that were off-limits for a long time for ethnographers (see Nader, 1969). And finally, it was human relations researchers who emphasized the value of studying interactional patterns and routines in the work context, anticipating the recent turn toward routines and practices in anthropological theory in general (see Ortner, 1984) and in the specific study of organizations and communities (see Schwartzman, 1989). In the following chapter the methodological implications of recent ethnographies of work and organizations by anthropologists are reviewed.

NOTES

1. There are actually two approaches to human relations research that can be identified. One approach is associated with industrial psychologists and, as discussed by Burrell and Morgan, this approach focuses on relationships between work, satisfaction, and performance and tends to favor experimental or quasi-experimental methods (1979, p. 143). The second human relations school is associated with the work of the researchers discussed in this chapter.

2. At the first meeting of the Society for Applied Anthropology, held at Harvard University in 1941, a number of papers on "industrial ethnology" were presented. The first two papers presented at this meeting concerned "The Application of Anthropology to Industry" (Arensberg) and "Organization Problems in Industry" (Chapple) (personal communication, F. L. W. Richardson, 1981).

4. STUDYING UP AND STUDYING DOWN

*How has it come to be . . . that anthropologists are more interested in why
peasants don't change than why the auto industry doesn't innovate, or why
the Pentagon or universities cannot be more organizationally creative?
The conservatism of such major institutions and bureaucratic organizations probably has wider implications for the species and for theories of
change than does the conservatism of peasantry.*

Laura Nader (1969, p. 289)

In the 1970s and 1980s an increasing number of anthropologists began
to turn their attention to the study of formal organizations and the place
of work in American society. Up until this time the study of work in
modern societies had received only sporadic attention from anthropologists, which is ironic because the discipline itself is centrally organized around the fieldwork experience. Some of the reasons for the neglect of organization and industry studies have already been discussed
in Chapter 3. In this Chapter I will examine recent studies of work and
organizations in American society and try to draw out the methodological implications of this research. The studies that have developed since
the 1970s may be viewed as both reactions to and extensions of the
human relations tradition begun by the Hawthorne research. I discuss
three types of studies that illustrate specific trends in research methods
as well as theoretical assumptions: (a) anthropology of work studies,
(b) organizational culture studies, and (c) the analysis of organizing processes (events, routines, gatherings) and their relation to larger systems.

The Anthropology of Work:
Shop Floors and World Systems

In 1969 in an article titled "Up the Anthropologist," Laura Nader
threw out a challenge to anthropologists: "What if, in reinventing anthropology, anthropologists were to study the colonizers, rather than the
colonized, the culture of power rather than the culture of the powerless,
the culture of affluence rather than the culture of poverty?" (p. 289). In
raising these questions she began to set an agenda for researchers
concerned with examining powerful institutions and organizations in
the United States as well as abroad, and the impact of these institutions
on the societies that anthropologists have traditionally studied. One of

the fields to respond to Nader's challenge is what has come to be known as anthropology of work studies.

Unlike the earlier human relations investigations, anthropology of work studies emphasize the importance of examining work and the workplace from a broader perspective. The place of formal organizations within the larger social and economic structure of modern class society is of particular interest to many researchers in this field (Britan & Cohen, 1980, p. 13). In several studies a neo-Marxist and/or materialist perspective and concern with political economy is apparent (e.g., Burawoy, 1979; Nash, 1979).

This research examines work in occupations and organizations such as factories, mines, automobile production, the garment industry, and the multinational corporation. Emphasis in these descriptions is given to the existence of conflict and alienation, exploitation of workers and worker response, and large power differentials between workers and management. In Wallman's terms "work is 'about' control—physical and psychological, social and symbolic" (1979, p. 1).[1] June Nash's (1981a) discussion of the impact of industrialization on work illustrates this approach:

> Whereas most members of the human species shared the ability to make and use tools during the Paleolithic and early Neolithic, as stratified societies developed, elites emerged who planned and organized the work of others. The trend is toward a narrowing scope for the application of the intelligence humans share as members of the same species.
>
> This trend has become acute with industrialization in the particular historical form in which it has developed. The debasement of most jobs to repetitive, short-cycle operations requiring little training and subject to managerial control eliminates the creative interaction that was the basis for human transformation. The concentration of decision-making and control is eliminating the variability and adaptability that were the principle advantages of the human species in evolution. Indeed, the capital intensive, high-energy conversion industrialization characteristic of monopoly capitalism may even eliminate the human input in production. The central problem for an applied anthropology of work is to find ways of improving the relationship between human potential and the productive process. (p. 3)

Anthropology of work studies emphasize the importance of using ethnography and also ethnohistory to develop new frameworks, which incorporate as central features the political and ideological dimensions of industrial concerns in order to make it easier to distinguish the "mists" of managerial rationalization and organization theory from the realities of corporate life (Burawoy, 1979, pp. 249-250). This approach expands analysis from the shop floor to include the nation-state as well as an all-inclusive world system, drawing for example on Wallerstein's (1974) world-system theory (see Nash, 1981b), or on evolutionary models and theories (see Wolfe, 1977). In the latter case, Wolfe presents a sociocultural evolutionary perspective on the development of supranational organizational systems and the increasing internationalization of production and economic activity.

Helen Safa (1986) illustrates this approach in her analysis of runaway shops and female employment in the garment industry in the United States. Using historical sources as well as anthropological methods, she outlines three stages in the labor recruitment process: "(1) Use of a native labor force, including recruitment from rural areas; (2) use of immigrant labor; and (3) the runaway shop. Each stage has used a different type of female labor force and has been characterized by a different pattern of capital accumulation" (p. 60). Her analysis examines the impact of these differences on women in the United States and in the Third World.

The world of multinational corporations and their impact on the United States and world economic systems is examined by June Nash (1979) in her article, "The Anthropology of the Multinational Corporation." Using interviews, participant observation, and historical analysis, she attempts to show how the spread of corporate power has been achieved at the cost of deepening national and regional schisms at a structural level and widening social and cultural disjunctions (p. 424). Nash uses research specifically focused on the position of global managers of "Monomer" (a petrochemical corporation) to examine this view, and she reports her surprise in discovering that the presumed "alienators" (i.e., management) are themselves alienated in their work because of a variety of forces and contradictions that effect their work life (e.g., increasing centralization of decision making, constant movement, acceleration of change): "What impressed me about the few middle managers I interviewed at length was the high degree of alienation they expressed in terms of the common indices of that condition: social isolation, powerlessness, meaninglessness, self-estrangement, and normlessness" (Nash, 1979, pp. 424-425).

Her analysis includes an examination of the recent history of the expansion of multinational corporations and the response to this expansion in the United States and abroad, the impact this expansion has had on the United States economy and shifts in the labor market, and also the formation of regional alliances such as OPEC. Monomer is examined at local, national, and international levels. The result of this study is the linking of the world of the global managers in a multinational corporation to the broad political and economic forces that both affect and are affected by these rapidly expanding corporate entities. This linking occurs theoretically by focusing on the existence and importance of material power differentials, inescapable interest conflicts, the development of alienation and the experience of oppression, and developing local, national, regional, and international schisms and disjunctions for interpreting individual and organizational behavior in these settings.

Nash's more recent research is on the restructuring of American industry from mass production to high-tech defense production, and the effect of this restructuring on families and communities.[2] Her specific focus is on the industrial city of Pittsfield, Massachusetts, and the General Electric corporation, which has dominated the economy of this city since 1903.[3] In formulating her analysis in *From Tank Town to High Tech* (1989), she is particularly concerned with the construction and maintenance of corporate hegemony and she uses Gramsci's definition of this phenomenon:

> [A]n order in which a certain way of life and thought is dominant, in which one concept of reality is diffused throughout society in all its institutional and private manifestation, informing with its spirit all taste, morality, customs, religious and political principles, and all social relations, particularly in their intellectual and moral connotations. (Gramsci in Nash, 1989, p. 11)

In this book she uses observations, interviews, collections of documents, and historical analyses to examine how the culture that workers in modern organizations "construct and reproduce in their daily lives is adapted to, and in turn affects, the operation of the global corporation in their community" (p.2).[4] She is specifically critical of studies of the labor process that are divorced from the wider society and portray workers as passive respondents to change. Her research seeks to counter these tendencies by portraying workers as active participants in the change processes that affect them. In this study she examines the region's economic history as well as corporate policy in order to understand the effect of industrial transformations on the lives of particular workers. She argues that corporate hegemony "is increasingly based on inputs from labor and professionals as well as corporate managers" (p. 12).

A second approach to the anthropological study of work is outlined by Gamst (1977). He argues for an "industrial ethnology," which focuses on the presentation of the "native's viewpoint and logic of classification" as well as the penetration and probing of the social reality beyond this "emic" perspective (pp. 3, 6). Gamst's study of "hoggers" illustrates this tradition, which might be more accurately labeled "occupational ethnography." In *The Hoghead* (1980), he uses his 6½ years of railroad engine service employment, as well as fieldwork and questionnaire data, to develop an ethnography of the rail world, from the perspective of the engineman on the Central City and Urbana Railroad. This ethnography begins with a description of a morning's work, from the perspective of the "hogger," and then the book provides detailed information on the enculturation of engineers, the formal and informal codes that guide their activities, and a typical run, beginning with the call and ending with heading home. But Gamst broadens these insider descriptions by examining the development of railroads in the United States, and also by depicting the extent and effect of current government regulations on railroad rules and the operations guided by these rules. The CC&U is now part of a multi-corporation conglomerate that invests heavily in non-railroad enterprises. The effect of being part of such a conglomerate, as well as the future of railroads in the United States (especially the debate over the nationalization of the railroads), are all examined in this book in order to present a study which Gamst considers to be "Warnerian" in its perspective and orientation.

Other occupational ethnographies that illustrate this approach include Herbert Applebaum's (1981) study of the culture of construction workers, William Pilcher's (1972) analysis of longshoremen, and John Van Maanen's (1973, 1977, 1979, 1982) in-depth descriptions of police work in Union City. This approach is also in line with the anthropology of work studies illustrated by Gamst (1980), but Van Maanen has used his fieldwork experiences to reflect in detail on both the problems and prospects of conducting organizational ethnography (see especially 1979). His goal in this research is "to uncover and explicate the ways in which people in particular work settings come to understand, account for, take action, and otherwise manage their day-to-day situation"

(1979, p. 540). Using his research experience with the police, Van Maanen shows the importance of distinguishing between first-order and second-order concepts in research (e.g., whose point of view is being represented, researcher or informant), differences between operational (the running stream of talk and activity) and presentational (informants' manufactured images) data, and the various ways of assessing the believability of the talk-based information collected (1979, pp. 540-548).

James P. Spradley and Brenda Mann illustrate a cognitive approach to the study of work and language following the fieldwork and interviewing principles of ethnoscience in *The Cocktail Waitress: Women's Work in a Man's Place* (1975). In this ethnography, Spradley and Mann focus specifically on the participants' knowledge of work in an American college bar, Brady's Bar. For example, distinguishing features of the *main bar* versus the *waitress station* versus the *telephone* are examined and discussed. To facilitate this research Mann became a waitress in this setting, and she illustrates how participant researchers use themselves as research instruments. After work, generally during debriefing conversations:

> [S]he [Mann] would try to find out what these experiences felt like, how she did things, what it felt like to work as a cocktail waitress. This kind of introspection of ordinary activities contrasts sharply with the ordinary participant who has learned to take the experience for granted. Introspection may not seem "objective," but it is a tool all of us use to understand new situations and to gain skill at following cultural rules. (Spradley, 1980, p. 57)

Larger cultural themes, which expressed themselves in specific verbal domains such as *places in the bar, kinds of employees,* and *kinds of customers,* were also examined in this research. Using the ethnoscientist's technique of componential analysis, it was found that an important dimension of contrast that occurred across these domains was concerned with gender or sex:

> Waitresses distinguished the places in the bar in terms of male space and female space; they distinguished kinds of employees primarily by gender; they distinguished drinks on the basis of male and female; customers also were divided up by male and female attributes. As we inspected these various domains, it became clear that an important aspect of cultural meaning was maleness and femaleness. A general principle or cultural

theme emerged: *Life in this bar should clearly demarcate male and female realms.* Once we discovered this theme, we began looking for other specific instances of this general principle. It turned out that even very small domains like *ways to tip* and *ways to pay for drinks* clearly expressed the theme of gender. (Spradley, 1980, p. 142)

The researchers use this study to make some general statements about the replication of cultural divisions between males and females in the context of a specific work setting. For example, they suggest that the work and roles of women in bars are an extension of their roles at home and elsewhere. "Like most institutions of American society, men hold sway at the center of social importance" (Spradley & Mann, 1975, p. 45). While this is certainly not a novel observation, what is novel about this study is the way that it illustrates the workings of social structure in a specific setting and the work of language in constituting and reflecting this structure.

Studying Organizational Culture

Although human relations researchers utilized the concept of culture in their studies of formal and informal organization, the current interest in the concept of culture for understanding organizational life has come not from anthropology but from the disciplines of psychology and business administration. In the business/management literature the concept of organizational culture appears to have been initially introduced in conjunction with attempts to understand how organizational *internal* environments might be conceptualized, assessed, and most important, controlled (see Deal & Kennedy, 1982).

Over the past several years, a variety of studies, some based on actual research and many presented as advice to managers, have appeared specifically on the subject of organizational culture. These studies and statements have been usefully reviewed by Smircich (1983) and more recently in a special issue of the *Anthropology of Work Review,* edited by Patricia Sachs (1989). Several approaches to the definition and study of organizational culture are identified in these reviews:

1. Culture as External Variable: The first approach comes from the field of comparative management, and in some ways is most compatible with traditional anthropological conceptions of culture. The research in this area treats culture as an external independent variable imported into the organization through its members (Smircich, 1983, p. 343). In this way culture is viewed as residing in geographic, linguistic, or ethnic groups. For example, researchers have sought to draw comparisons between French and American managers and conceptions of organizational structure (Inzerelli & Laurent, in Smircich, 1983). Other studies adopting this orientation are Whyte's (1969) analysis of leadership, types of supervisory relationships, and worker satisfaction in Japan, Peru, and the United States, as well as the more well-known comparisons of Japanese and American management style (e.g., Ouchi, 1981).

There are many theoretical and methodological problems associated with this research tradition and these have been criticized by Roberts (1970, also see Weinshall, 1970). Perhaps one of the most serious flaws of this approach is that, while it appears to be sensitive to cultural issues, it is essentially ethnocentric. As Roberts suggests, "currently, the questions asked bear a 'made in USA' stamp. They examine organizational behavior in other cultures from an American point of view" (p. 87), and as is true of much of the interest in organizational culture, the American point of view is actually an American manager's point of view.

2. Culture as Informal Organization: A second approach treats culture as something that develops within an organization, and here culture is equated with "informal" organization conceptualized as the expressive and non-job-related aspects of organizational life. Pacanowsky and O'Donnell-Trujillo (1982) illustrate this approach to the study of organizational culture:

> The jumping off point for this approach is the mundane observation that more things are going on in organizations than getting the job done. People do get the job done . . . but people in organizations also gossip, joke, knife one another, initiate romantic involvements, cue new employees on ways of doing the least amount of work that still avoids hassles from a supervisor, talk sports and arrange picnics. Now it seems to us quite a presumption that work activities should have some kind of ascendant hold on our attention, whereas picnic arranging should not. (pp. 116-117)

Studies mounted from this perspective have focused attention on the study of organizational values, as these may be created or transmitted by organizational myths, stories, and legends (Boje, Fedor, & Rowland, 1982; Martin, Feldman, Hatch & Sitkin, 1983; Tommerup, 1988); jokes, rituals, and ceremonies (Deal & Kennedy, 1982); and symbols and special-ized language (Andrews & Hirsch, 1983)—although I have not found any specific studies of picnic arranging. In these investigations culture is viewed as "shared key values and beliefs," and researchers seek to examine and understand how shared understandings, meanings, norms, and values are developed within specific organizational settings (Jelinck, Smircich, & Hirsch, 1983, p. 331; Smircich, 1983, p. 345). This approach also appears to assume that one can discover an organizational culture that unifies behavior and, once understood, can be molded and shaped by management to further their ends (Smircich, 1983, p. 346). This particular assumption has been examined and critiqued by Baba (1989).

3. Culture as Formal and Informal Organization: A third group of studies questions the assumption that culture somehow resides only in informal or expressive activities in organizations. This approach is more directly connected with recent anthropological studies of organizations and has been articulated by Kathleen Gregory in an article in *Administrative Science Quarterly.* She suggests that applying the

> anthropological approach in corporations leads one to study participants' views about all aspects of the corporate experience. These would include the work itself, the technology, the formal organization structure, the everyday language, not only myths, stories or special jargon. That some researchers select these for special emphasis says more about the culture of the researchers than the researched, for whom all culture is equally taken for granted. (1983, p. 359)

This statement illustrates an important difference in orientation exhibited in the literature on organizational culture that is developing now within anthropology (see Sachs, 1989; Sibley, 1986) as well as in other disciplines. On the one hand, there are researchers who are attempting to use the concept of culture to solve the problems of management and to improve "the bottom line." On the other hand, researchers have also begun to use this concern with the bottom line and with management problems as a way to examine and understand the culture of managers as well as organizations in American society. This approach recognizes that anthropologists must both understand and work within native cultural systems, but they must also question and attempt to go beyond them by adopting a comparative and critical perspective in their research.

Gregory argues specifically for the use of "native view paradigms," and especially ethnoscience ethnography, as a way to examine the multiple perspectives and cultures of informants in detail. Her research was conducted among computer technical professionals in Silicon Valley computer companies, and since this area is so multifaceted and rapidly changing she decided that "it seemed most appropriate to discover how participants made sense of it themselves" (1983, p. 366). A major emphasis was given to learning native concepts for social categories, and she discusses in detail the value of ethnoscience interviewing techniques for understanding these concepts. She also illustrates how these native conceptions can be displayed, compared, and understood. For example, Figure 4.1 illustrates how one informant makes distinctions between kinds of computer product development companies. In contrast to many organizational culture studies, Gregory was concerned with representing cultures as they are, rather than how managers might wish them to be (1983, p. 63).

The importance of understanding the significance of the cultural units that informants create for themselves is also illustrated by Gregory's study (1984). In this case she found that "the project" was the most important unit of interaction for computer professionals, overriding in a variety of ways the company itself. Her research documents how "the project" organizes interaction, as well as focus and commitment for individuals, and is therefore crucial for understanding the experience of working in this profession.

A Turn Toward Routines: From Organizations to Organizing

Gregory's interest in the native construction of work and the interactional occasions, such as "the project," which constitute work, illustrates one of the most recent interests of organizational researchers and anthropologists. Karl Weick argues for the value of this approach in the field of organizational behavior by stressing the need for researchers to focus on the *organizing* processes out of which a sense of organization unfolds and is enacted, instead of continuing to examine organizations as objective, concrete, material, and unproblematic entities. Weick suggests that the basic theme for his *organizing model* is found in the recipe for sense-making, which he describes as follows:

> "How can I know what I think until I see what I say?" Organizations are presumed to talk to themselves over and over to find out what they're

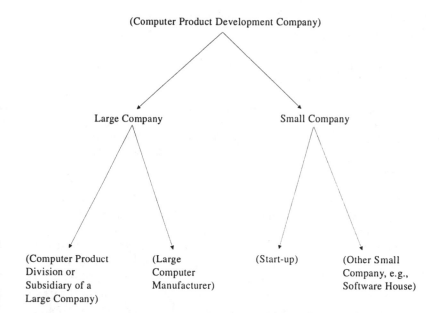

Figure 4.1. Taxonomy of "Kinds of Computer Product Development Companies," a Segment of One Interviewee's Lexical/Semantic Field.

NOTE: From "Native-View Paradigms: Multiple Cultures and Cultural Conflicts in Organizations" by K. Gregory, 1983, *Administrative Science Quarterly*, 28 (3), p. 368, Figure 1. © Copyright 1983 by *Administrative Science Quarterly*. Reprinted by permission.

thinking. . . . The organism or group enacts equivocal raw talk, the talk is viewed retrospectively, sense is made of it, and then this sense is stored as knowledge in the retention process. The aim of each process has been to reduce equivocality and to get some idea of what has occurred. (1979, pp. 133-134)

This approach also requires challenging the assumption that researchers focus on the production of *either* micro- or macro-level studies. In going beyond this micro/macro-level dichotomy, McDermott and Roth (1978) argue that interactional research (presumably a micro-level approach) consistently shows how detailed analysis of everyday "ordinary behavior" and occasions and routines "can reveal much of the machinery for the workings of social structure" (p. 323). In other words, macro-level forces and constraints are, in fact, observable at the interactional level, where these forces have meaning for individuals in their everyday lives:

> This way of proceeding offers us the most empirical documentation of how the social world is ordered; as such it tells us a great deal about what traditionally has been called the social order, namely, the organization of interactional—communicative, institutional, and material—resources people have available for ordering their behavior with each other. With this approach there are no macro and micro constraints, no macro or micro behaviors, but people leaning on each other in specifiable contexts. (pp. 323-324)

The most recent call for a turn to the everyday is from researchers with a practice orientation (see Ortner, 1984, and especially Bourdieu, 1977; Giddens, 1984). As Giddens suggests in presenting his theory of structuration, "All social systems, no matter how grand or far-flung, both express and are expressed in the routines of daily social life . . ." (p. 36). Organizational researchers have been slow to realize the value of examining the "everyday routines" that make up organizational life because, for the most part, these routines have been either taken for granted (like meetings) or dismissed as unimportant. In contrast some researchers have begun to realize that routines and forms like meetings and stories (discussed below) provide researchers with important information about the social structure and culture of organizations and society.

Interpreting Meetings

Nothing could be more commonplace than meetings in organizations, but researchers have chosen to look behind rather than at meetings. In the West we believe that meetings should exemplify our basic values of pragmaticism, task orientation, efficiency, and rationality. We are frustrated when we find that meetings do not seem to accomplish or display these values. The classic joke about the functioning of committees as meeting groups: "A camel is a horse assembled by a committee," reflects this folk wisdom about meetings, but the research literature makes use of it as well. In general, three orientations have been taken toward meetings (see Schwartzman, 1989, for a more detailed discussion of these orientations): (a) Meetings are viewed as *tools* for tasks and researchers have used them to study other things (e.g., leadership in groups, the effect of group size on group performance, testing decision models); (b) meetings are evaluated as ineffective tools and treated as either the symptoms of or cure for a host of organizational problems (e.g., Drucker, 1974); and (c) researchers and managers, frequently working together, attempt to "fix" meetings (e.g., "How to" books, such as Dunsing, 1978).

One important assumption that ties these orientations together is the view that there is (or should be) a tight connection between individual (or group) intentions and action (March & Olsen, 1976, p. 19).[5] If something happens that interferes with this relationship—meetings would be a good example, according to many people—then it is the event or the form that must be fixed. Clarity and connection between action and intention are important values that have made it very difficult to see meetings as anything other than a nuisance, a bore, or a very bad joke (remember, "a camel is a horse assembled by a committee").

In order to make meetings a topic as opposed to a tool of research, I have suggested elsewhere (Schwartzman, 1989) that we need to re-imagine meetings and that we can use anthropology, especially research on political language, to do this. An anthropology of meetings conceptualizes meetings as communication events that must be examined because they are embedded within a sociocultural setting (an organization, a community, a society) as a constitutive social form. The approach described here is motivated by an appreciation of the idea that the world does not appear to us as formalized concepts (such as structure or culture, or hierarchy and value), but only in particular routines and gatherings, composed of specific actors (or agents) attempting to press their claims on one another and trying to make sense of what is happening to them. In this way it is possible to see how the process of meeting contributes to the production and reproduction of the structures of everyday life. However, while meetings are accomplishing this, these structures are interpreted and experienced as objective entities that are external and unrelated to these actions and occasions. In this way meetings have been pushed out of the picture when, in fact, from this perspective, they are partly responsible for creating it.

In conjunction with this view, it is necessary to recognize that situations, routines, and gatherings are themselves "practical accomplishments," as the ethnomethodologists have demonstrated repeatedly. These events are constructed by actors and researchers out of what is frequently "a blooming, buzzing confusion," and whatever order is achieved is always precarious and tentative. Meetings, as Myers (1986) reminds us in a study of the Pintupi in Australia, are "delicate achievements" but they are achievements in every society. Meetings are involved in the construction and imposition of order in individuals' lives in ways that have been generally unappreciated by participants and researchers. However, I suggest that meetings are responsible for the construction of both order and disorder in social systems, and so they must be conceptualized as occasions with both conservative (as sense-makers and social and cultural validators) and transformative capacities (see Schwartzman, 1989).

SEEING WITH MEETINGS

The relationship of individuals to organizational or environmental constraints, which are (or may become) limiting and constraining, is a problematic feature of all discussions of action and structure. In my view it is important to emphasize that individuals do not and cannot act outside of forms such as communication events like meetings, which they use to generate interaction as well as to interpret what it means (*we are greeting each other, we are bargaining, we are playing, we are meeting*). It is in these forms, and only in these forms, that individuals are able to transact, negotiate, strategize, and attempt to realize their specific aims, but cultural systems and social structures are "bred into" these forms, as Ranson, Hinings, and Greenwood (1980) suggest. It was my gradual understanding of this point that helped me realize that I could only portray the experience of working, as well as conducting research, at a community mental health center ("Midwest") *through* the meetings (I called them *key meetings*), which informants used to make sense of or "see" the organization and their actions in it. In this particular context staff and board members saw their world as a battleground and they became caught up in a battle for control, while at the same time viewing one another's activities as "out of control." In my view staff and board members saw the organization and their actions quite differently because they were seeing events, and trying to understand and interpret them, through different meetings (staff meetings versus board meetings). To explain these differences in terms of the different roles individuals occupied in the organization does not help us understand how these differences were experienced and generated in the daily actions of individuals in this context.

Individuals also use meetings to read and/or see their place in particular social systems. We say that an individual is or is not a powerful person, but often we only "know" this based on how we read and interpret events in a meeting. This was certainly the case for participants at Midwest, where there were very few ways outside of meetings for individuals to negotiate and/or determine their status and social ranking, and where their status was frequently in flux. In some cases it was only by astutely "reading" meetings (e.g., who knows about, was/was not attending, calling/canceling, arriving or leaving, and so on) that an individual might learn about his or her place in the status system of the Center.

SEEING WITH MEETINGS AT MIDWEST[6]

It was not an easy task to arrange a meeting at Midwest because many participants recognized the implications of agreeing to meet with one another. In some instances individuals would flatly refuse to meet because of what acceptance of this form meant, in terms of recognizing and legitimizing social relationships and cultural values. However, even when individuals did agree to meet with one another, it was no easy matter to arrange the meeting because of each individual's meeting and appointment commitments. In this case meeting negotiations tended to focus on setting the meeting time. A brief interchange of a meeting negotiation illustrates the difficulty Center actors experienced in attempting to set the time for a formal meeting. This interchange also illustrates the wealth and range of information communicated in such a negotiation. This particular event is taken from a tape made of a special grievance committee meeting. In this case, representatives of board and staff were meeting about an employee grievance, but because of their need to read another report, they found it necessary to break the original meeting frame in an attempt to schedule another meeting.

MA: I would like to see as the schedule, and if we can swing this, you and I will have that report by noon from Carol. We will spend Monday afternoon reviewing, copies should be made to everybody involved, and even I will have drawn conclusions by, hopefully, Monday evening. And we should be ready for a meeting Tuesday if the time allows. For everybody present. Is that fair?

BG: I don't know. Because Monday night we have a steering committee meeting, and then there's always lots of stuff to do on Mondays. We need like—I would prefer to have some time Tuesday morning. Whatever we can do Monday afternoon, but I need some time Tuesday morning, 'cause I don't know what all, you know—whenever there's a meeting—

VH: Why don't you notify us, notify Carol and me, when you've reached your final conclusions on this and we'll set up meeting as soon as we can thereafter.

MA: I would like to take a block of time, because I know how hard it is to get everybody to meet—

BG: We could do it like Tuesday—if it's like mid to late Tuesday afternoon, that's OK.

MA: Yeah. Either that or Wednesday morning perhaps, one of the two times. Tuesday afternoon? You're shaking your head.

DS: I can't make it Wednesday. I can't make it Thursday.

MA: Can you make it Tuesday afternoon around—

DS: Not if there's going to be a MHD negotiating meeting.

MA: Is there?

PR: There will be people meeting. I do not know how long they will meet. . . . I think we ought to plan it for, and notify people for, any time from 3:30 on. Depending on—

DS: MHD meeting Tuesday.

PR: Depending on what happens with the MHD meeting. It may not go any length of time whatsoever. On the other hand, it may require our attendance. There are plenty of those people who can be there without us. In the event that we can't make it at all on Tuesday, when would be our alternative time?

(Background talk, mostly inaudible)

PR: Wednesday and Thursday are the—

MA: You mean that's the other meeting?

PR: Yeah.

MA: I wasn't invited. Friday morning?

PR: How come I'm not going to go?

MA: You want to go?

PR: I don't know.

DS: Monday we'll decide that.

MA: How about Friday morning?

BG: If not Tuesday afternoon.

MA: If not Tuesday afternoon, then Friday morning will be the next best time as I see it.

PR: When's the NAS meeting?
FE: Friday morning.
MB: Yes.
MA: I think we should set a goal of Tuesday. That's for sure.

This excerpt illustrates several aspects of the meetings at Midwest, including how the seemingly inconsequential, although often annoying, process of arranging a scheduled meeting contains innumerable possibilities for displaying as well as finding out about one's status in an organization (e.g., whose time takes precedence in setting a meeting, who needs to be there and who does not, who knows about which meetings, and so on). In the process of negotiating a meeting, other meetings would frequently be used as a dodge or excuse to get out of a meeting one did not want to attend, or to see how important one's presence really was in terms of whether the meeting negotiation could continue without his or her participation. Along with this, once a meeting time was set, the organizer might cancel it because of other "pressing" matters, or an individual might cancel out of a specific meeting for the same reason, and all of these actions were effective markers of status at the Center. As the above example illustrates, meetings were important for seeing one's place in the organization.

Interpreting Stories

Stories and storytelling are common activities that individuals in all organizations use to make sense of their world and their life at work. For the most part, however, we take stories (just like meetings) for granted —we may tell them, laugh at them, and even be horrified by them, but mostly we do not take these accounts very seriously. Stories make their appearance in conversations, interviews, informal discussions, and other events in a variety of ways. A story might be an account of something that happened in the distant past or only a few minutes earlier, and they are typically presented as examples of particular points (e.g., "I'll give you an example of how we do things here. One day . . . " story follows). In general, stories in organizations are told as if they depict real events, and they are heard and repeated as representations of real events.

The significance of stories in contemporary organizational settings has recently come to the attention of a few researchers concerned with examining organizational behavior and culture (e.g., Clark, 1972; Martin, Feldman, Hatch, & Sitkin, 1983; Mattingly, 1989, 1991; Myerhoff, 1978; Pacanowsky & O'Donnell-Trujillo, 1982; Peters & Waterman, 1982; Schwartzman, 1984; Tommerup, 1988). This research suggests that stories are an important form for: (a) communicating historical experiences and providing individuals with a way to weave this experience into discussions of current activities; (b) distinguishing one's organization as the best and/or worst and also for stereotyping other organizations; (c) socializing new members into an organization; (d) documenting successes and failures and drawing conclusions (morals) from these examples; (e) indirectly communicating information to individuals about a range of issues that may be too sensitive or threatening to discuss directly; and, finally, (f) stories may be most important because they shape and sustain individuals' images of the organization in which they work. It is in this way that stories play an important role in constituting an organizational reality for participants. What it is important to emphasize here is that in many organizations, there may be several organizational realities. The stories one hears and tells, and the morals that are drawn from them, go a long and generally unrecognized way toward constituting these realities. Ethnographers can learn a great deal about the structure and culture of an organization by paying attention to the stories that organizational members relate to one another as well as to researchers.

The continual narration of organizational stories can shape and reshape the way the individuals experience their organization. This was definitely the case at Midwest, where stories generated a series of recurring images that individuals used to depict their activities and relationships, especially their conflictual relationships. The image of the "crazy" organization was a powerful one for individuals in this organization and it influenced the way they both described and experienced their work at Midwest. As already mentioned, staff and board members were in conflict with each other, and each group told stories about the other group that highlighted their problems, incompetence, and "craziness." These stories simultaneously created, transformed, and commented on the realities of Center life. Bill, a staff member at Midwest, tells a story in an interview about the most recent "crazy" board meeting that he attended:

You won't believe the last board meeting I went to, it was one of those coalitions of community control . . . This young woman . . . delivers a sensible, a little bit adolescent in the sense that she wasn't as articulate as she could have been, request to become a member of the Council, and there is a member of the board who you might have thought they were talking about recognizing the People's Republic as opposed to Formosa . . . I was unable to follow the thought/cognitive function that she was laying down verbally, even given the fact that it was not germane to [the other woman's request] . . . Mary [another member of the board] was trying to say, slow down . . . this doesn't make any sense. Then Mary made a motion, which was weird enough, so they had to discuss it for 15 to 20 minutes. And sure enough when that woman left [the one making the membership request], she didn't have any idea where she had been and she walked out without her coat and purse. Five minutes later out on the street she realized she left her clothes behind. It was like that woman must have felt like she was on a teeter-totter that not only was going up and down, but was being spun at some tremendous rate, because that was one of the craziest [meetings] I've even been to.

Summary: Micro/Macro Ethnographies

In anthropology, Marcus and Fisher argue that one of the challenges for researchers is "how to represent the embedding of richly described local cultural worlds in larger impersonal systems of political economy" (1986, p. 77). This interest in examining how local cultural worlds are embedded in larger systems of political economy requires that researchers turn their attention toward the study of organizations, bureaucracies, and bureaucratization (as argued persuasively by Nader in 1969, and later by Handelman in 1978). However, when anthropologists turn their attention to these issues, then the assumption that there are small-scale "personal" cultural worlds versus large-scale "impersonal" forces and systems of political economy must also be challenged. In fact, what is required is an examination of the interaction between the local cultural worlds, which anthropologists have traditionally studied, and the local cultural worlds of bureaucrats, bureaucracies, industries, and organizations, which anthropologists have begun to realize (actually re-realize) they must understand. This requires that anthropologists "study up," while it also requires that political economists and other researchers "study down" developing ways "to rebuild understanding of macro-level systems from the bottom up" (Marcus & Fisher 1986: 80). Ethnography is crucial here because as a method for research it problematicizes the ways that individuals and groups constitute organizations (and societies) on a daily interactional basis. In the following chapter I will discuss some of the methods that organizational ethnographers use to problematicize, describe, and interpret the local cultural worlds of organizations.

NOTES

1. Wallman (1979) presents a useful perspective on and introduction to the social anthropology of work, in an edited volume that includes case studies of Israeli and Canadian dockworkers, labor relations on South African farms, sweepers in Banares, and the work of a group of social workers (family pedagogues) within the Swedish bureaucracy. The monograph does not include case study material from the United States, but it provides an important comparative perspective on the topic, which is missing in many of the psychological and sociological studies of work.

2. See also the interesting work of Katherine Newman (*Falling from Grace: The Meaning of Downward Mobility in American Culture,* 1988) on the lay-offs of Singer Sewing Machine workers in Elizabeth, New Jersey. Nash suggests that Newman's research documents the tendency of Singer workers to criticize themselves for their inability to compete with Japanese workers, whereas the Pittsfield workers she studied were more likely to criticize management tactics directly (1989, p. 325).

3. There are a number of interesting parallels between the transformation and changes in Pittsfield and the transformation of the Hawthorne plant (as part of the Western Electric company and the AT&T company) and the community of Cicero and western Chicago.

4. Nash interviewed a variety of individuals in the community of Pittsfield. For example, she interviewed women and men who had organized the labor movement at General Electric, individuals in women's organizations and the peace movement, spokespersons for General Electric, owners and managers of other corporations and companies in the city, and also conducted interviews that focused "on the work histories of 100 workers on the International Union of Electrical Workers (IUE) active and laid-off lists" (1989, p. 2).

5. James March and Johan Olsen's work on organizational decision making (e.g., 1976) is interesting for anthropologists to consider because it challenges the folk-models embedded in our theories about organizations, models that privilege decisions (as tasks) and individual intention in attempting to explain how choices are made in these systems.

6. Adapted from Schwartzman (1989, pp. 119-121).

5. FIELDWORK ROLES AND
FIELDWORK PROCESSES

When [anthropologist] Kathleen Gregory Huddleston of the University of California at Irvine showed up at a Silicon Valley computer maker, she was greeted by a group of excited engineers who handed her a grab bag of cultural artifacts: a collection of Xerox art, a gag gift brochure of the company's products, and a recording of Silicon Valley Guy, a Valley Girl-like spoof of computerspeak. The gifts, says Huddleston, were presented only partly in jest, because the engineers "really did think of themselves as exotic." So she took them seriously in her study.

Sana Siwalop (1986, p. 172)

Since the Hawthorne research established a tradition of using social science disciplines to study organizations, researchers have adopted a range of roles and methods for investigating problems as diverse as relations between workers and foremen on assembly lines, the interactions of department store salespeople, the social system of a mental hospital, the work culture of computer technical professionals, the effect of industrial restructuring on workers and communities, and storytelling in a corporate setting. The literature discussed in the previous chapters illustrates the variety of roles that ethnographers have adopted, beginning with the role of *management consultant*, first used by anthropologists in the Hawthorne research. Anthropologists have also adopted the role of *cultural broker*, attempting to understand and sometimes mediate conflicts between groups with differing interests and cultures in organizational systems. Anthropologists have also used their ethnographic skills to work as *scribes*, documenting the organization worlds and meaning systems of particular groups, and finally, anthropologists have also acted as *critics* of organizations and the social and economic systems of which they are a part. Sometimes these roles evolve and change over time, during the course of a project, but they may also be related to the theoretical paradigm that the researcher uses. In adopting these roles for specific fieldwork situations, ethnographers have also adapted their methods to the demands of fieldworking in complex organizations. In this chapter I review the process of conducting ethnographic fieldwork, using the experiences of the researchers reviewed in the previous chapters. James Spradley (1980) makes an important distinction between cyclical and linear research styles. Ethnography is cyclical because the major tasks (like asking questions, recording observations, and analyzing data) are repeated over and over again (pp. 26, 28). There are, however, certain stages that most ethnographers do go through in the process of conducting a study. This chapter is organized according to these stages of fieldwork.

Access, Entry, and First Encounters

Everything counts.

H. L. Goodall (1989, p. xv)

Stepping into a setting for the first time is probably the most significant phase of the entire ethnographic process. This is especially true when working within one's own society. For a long time many researchers regarded the problems of access and the experience of first encounters as "noise," as far as data/information for the research project was concerned. These experiences were viewed as something to negotiate and get out of the way, rather than as data valuable in their own right. In contrast, I believe that access issues (i.e., the process of seeking permission and approval for research) and first encounters provide researchers with a rich source of data. It is in these encounters that the most dramatic differences between the ethnographer's culture and the informant's culture will be apparent. The surprises, differences, misunderstandings, and such that occur in these encounters may foreshadow major research concerns and issues; however, in the beginning, researchers may not know how to interpret what these differences reveal about themselves and their informants. This is why it is extremely important to take detailed field notes in the beginning of one's fieldwork. June Nash (1989) reports that she followed the advice of Sol Tax at the University of Chicago when she began her research in Pittsfield, Massachusetts, with General Electric. It was his view that it was in the early days of fieldwork that "commonplace behaviors still strike one as peculiar. The shock of experiencing different ways of thinking and behaving wears off as one becomes accustomed to them" (Nash, 1989, p. 2).

First encounters are also the first time that informants and researchers have to observe each other. No matter what role one tries to adopt in the fieldwork situation, in the beginning informants will make sense of the researcher in the way that they make sense of all other strangers who appear and begin to ask many questions. For this reason organizational ethnographers have been seen as evaluators, consultants, federal investigators, spies from other companies or agencies, and journalists. Most settings are not familiar with ethnographic research, and therefore it takes some time for informants and researchers both to understand what each is up to and to label the behavior in an appropriate way. It is also important to recognize that while researchers are watching informants, informants are also watching researchers. Peter Blau experienced this problem in his first field research. In the government agency he studied, he was suspected of being a member of the Hoover Commission, which carried out investigations of various branches of the federal government at the time of his research (1963, p. 277). Blau also reports on the problem of failing to realize that his definition of the beginning of his project, which actually began after he had already been at the agency for 2 weeks familiarizing himself with its operations, was not the same definition as that held by his informants:

> What I failed to realize is that what I defined as the beginning of the actual observation was not the beginning for these agents. I had been seen around for two weeks, and my failure explicitly to clarify my identity earlier had given rumors about me that much time to circulate. The private office and my preoccupation with becoming familiar with a complex bureaucratic structure had blinded me to the fact that I was already being observed by these agents, even though I had not started observing them. (1963, p. 278)

The importance of first encounters was brought home to me in my study of Midwest Community Mental Health Center. When I initiated the project with a team of social scientists working for a state mental health research department, we were initially perceived as spies for the state, which provided a significant source of funding for this Center. Although this seemed like a strange conclusion from our point of view, it made sense in terms of the Center's experience with the State Mental Health Department's continuous monitoring and evaluation procedures. At Midwest it took approximately 6 months of active negotiations, beginning with a letter and ending with meetings with board members, before we were allowed to present our project to the entire executive board. This presentation led to an approximately one-hour discussion, which ranged over issues of purpose, confidentiality, staff time, who we "really" were, and statements of support from staff and board members. At the conclusion of this meeting we were granted approval to begin the project.

This was a very tense time for the researchers because we felt that we had invested a great deal of time and effort into the access negotiations, and we really could not predict how they would turn out. Of course we were very pleased when our project was finally approved, but we were then told that we must present our study to the staff in 2 days to secure their support. Immediately we began to worry about this meeting. An excerpt from my field notes, written after this first meeting, reflects my concern as well as surprise about the events at this first meeting with staff:

> After 6 months of access negotiations we have finally been granted permission to begin our study of Midwest. Our first meeting with staff (2 days after the Council meeting) occurred today (Wednesday) during the regularly scheduled staff meeting held in what I believe is called the "hub" at the "barn" (which I think is what the Center's main building on Harding Avenue and Central is called). We were *very* apprehensive about this meeting because we thought that our presence and purpose might become a focus of controversy for staff and we would be denied access, but we were *very* surprised (and relieved) by the response to our presentation. We passed out copies of our outline, which people didn't seem to read. I briefly presented our research project by discussing the nature of the research, the potential value of the research, and our relation to the State Mental Health Department. There was only one question, concerning how much time we would be at the Center. Following our presentation, staff continued their staff meeting, and became very involved in listening and responding to a report about a recent statement from the board, which essentially seemed to say that Center staff should not be "in therapy" with other Center staff.
>
> There was a great deal of very agitated discussion about this issue, including problems with defining what is therapy, who was a therapist, and especially the issue of how (or whether) one could distinguish between therapy and supervision. There were many side comments around the table (most of which I could not hear). One person, I think her name was Sheila, seemed to dominate the discussion and she was very skillful and articulate in speaking. Paul Chase, the acting director, was technically in charge of the meeting. The results of this discussion seemed to be to bring these issues of staff and therapy back to the board to ask for clarification. . . . After this meeting one of the staff said to me that he still wasn't convinced that "you bug-collectors should be here."

One of the things that I later realized was how so many of the interests, issues, and interpretations that we developed in this research were foreshadowed in these notes. For example, all of our first encounters, except the initial letters, were in meetings and it was *the meeting* that later became the subject of my research and the focus of the book I wrote about this Center (see Schwartzman, 1989). The recurring conflict and confusion over who could be a proper patient, and what it meant to be staff at the Center, was an important theme in the culture of this agency and this conflict is clearly reflected in my notes about this meeting. In fact, this conflict overrode the staff's concern about our presence at the Center, which accounts for my surprise when we were only asked one question and then staff moved on to the issue that was most salient to them at that moment (the therapy issue). Finally, the importance of Sheila as an informal leader at the Center, and her opposition to Paul Chase (the formal leader), was also clearly reflected in these notes, and this also turned out to be an important piece of information about the social structure and hierarchy of this organization.

The importance of how one presents oneself to gatekeepers in an organization is also crucial for setting up particular expectations about one's research, and even for gaining entry into a setting. W. F. Whyte (1984) reports on his struggles with gaining access to settings when he began his study of restaurants in 1944. He was helped in part by Vernon Stouffer, who was a member of the National Restaurant Association committee that was sponsoring the project, and so the Chicago Loop Stouffers became the first case study (pp. 60-61). However, when trying to convince other owners or managers to become a part of the study, he found that they had one of two responses, either things were so fine that a study was not needed or things were so bad that it would be dangerous to bring in an outsider.

> Frustrated in the direct approach, I adopted a different strategy. After an initial explanation of the nature of the study, I asked the restaurateur to tell me how things were going in his or her restaurant and what problems should be given special attention in our study. As the discussion proceeded, with the restaurateur doing most of the talking, I would find openings to relate similar problems or experiences from other restaurants we were studying. Without pressing the point, I would add that we were then considering further restaurants for case studies and had a number of possibilities in mind. On my first try with this strategy, the restaurateur asked if we would be willing to study his establishment, After a moment of apparent indecision, I agreed. (p. 61)

Roles and Research

The first task of an organizational ethnographer is to try to understand what cultural knowledge, behavior, and artifacts participants share and use to interpret their experiences (Spradley, 1980, pp. 10, 30-31). The various roles that researchers assume in settings will partly determine how well they are able to carry out this task. When researchers enter the organization as management consultants or culture brokers, they are usually brought into the setting with the explicit purpose of solving particular problems, generally management problems.[1] This makes it difficult to broaden the scope of one's inquiry, although it is frequently necessary because in order to exploit the serendipitous quality of ethnography, researchers need to be able to "describe cultures as they are before assessing how they should be" (Gregory, 1983, p. 363) or before they try to "fix" them.[2] For this reason some human relations researchers (with the explicit purpose of describing and inscribing culture) chose to adopt a covert research role in order to better describe the work groups they were studying. Donald Roy (1952, 1953, 1954, 1959) produced a variety of insightful analyses of work group relationships and adaptations by taking a job in a machine shop in Chicago that produced railway jacks. He is particularly well known for his studies of output restriction, the phenomenon first examined in the Bank Wiring Observation Room, and for illustrating how this process can be a rational response to management irrationality (Burawoy, 1979, p. 51). In conducting his research, however, he chose not to inform either management or workers of his research intentions in order to remain "one of the boys on the line" (Roy, 1952, p. 427). In contrast, in 1974 Michael Burawoy began work as a machine operator in what turned out to be the same factory, now taken over by another company, that Roy had worked in 30 years earlier. He chose to inform workers of his research intentions, although he notes that they "regarded my enterprise with a mixture of disbelief and amusement. Some couldn't understand why there wasn't an easier way of obtaining a degree than by working in a factory for a year" (Burawoy, 1979, p. xv).

In one of the most well-known covert studies of a group of organizations, Melville Dalton conducted research in four firms, in an attempt "to get as close as possible to the world of managers and to interpret this world and its problems from the inside, as they are seen and felt at various points and levels" (1959, p. 1). He chose not to seek formal permission from management, but instead took on specific staff positions and then selectively informed individuals of a generalized research interest. Dalton's overall interest was in trying to understand "the schisms and ties between official and unofficial action" and he relied heavily on information from "intimates"—individuals who knew generally about his research interests; work diaries (which recorded his observations about events, biographical information, gossip, information on unusual incidents, clique activities); and documents he had access to, such as personnel files, grievance records, and minutes of meetings (pp. 162-164).

All of my research in organizations has been conducted using an overt research role, although in some instances I have taken on working roles in particular settings. For example, when studying a day-care center I took on the role of a volunteer, an activity that was practiced by other individuals in the setting. Although the teachers and other staff treated me as a volunteer, the children almost always related to me as a teacher. In studying the mental health center, we defined ourselves very clearly as researchers and, as described above, it took quite a long time to negotiate access to this setting as researchers. Once we were granted permission to study the center, however, we seemed to be immediately accepted by staff and for the most part were related to as if we were staff, even though we did not perform staff functions and continually reminded individuals of our research role.

The kind of role that one adopts will also determine what kinds of methods one will be able to use. For example, researchers who work covertly will not be able to formally interview informants; as Dalton remarks, "I did little formal interviewing because of the obvious problem of explaining what I was doing and the inadequacy of the approach for getting at unofficial activities" (p. 163). In contrast, researchers who work overtly tend to worry that they will not observe natural behavior or that things will be hidden from them. Of course this happens, but it is very difficult to hide culture although it may be partially out of the awareness of one's informants. Making the implicit explicit then becomes one of the goals of organizational ethnography.

Context Analysis

All of the groups that an organizational ethnographer may study will be composed of specific individuals with particular roles, interacting with each other in specific occasions. Depending upon the size and complexity of an organization, just trying to describe and characterize the various parties and gatherings that make up a setting can itself be a daunting task. One approach that I have found to be useful in studies of both small and large organizations is what I refer to as context analysis.

Using a grid format it is possible to identify the range and type of organizational participation and interaction that characterizes an organization, agency, program, and the like. It is also possible to include the researcher in this interaction format, and in this way recognize not only what role the investigator is playing in the setting but also what contexts include or exclude him or her. This is also a useful way to examine which contexts lend themselves to observations or interviews or some combination of both, especially in the early stages of research, and which contexts one wants to learn more about. Figure 5.1 utilizes this approach to illustrate the variety of communication contexts for program actors in a play therapy program conducted at a day-care center. The *patients* in this program were 8 of the 40 children attending Eastside Day Care Center during the time of the program. Program *staff* consisted of three play therapists who worked for the community agency conducting the program. Program *management* was undertaken by one supervisor at the community agency, whose director acted as *sponsor* of the program by allocating agency staff and funds (a combination of state and city mental health funds) to it. The program's intended *clients* were the Eastside Day Care Center teachers and administrators. The program *researcher* was myself.

The program culture was mediated in part by the multiple communication or actor interaction contexts that the program's structure created (See Schwartzman, 1983). Referring to Figure 5.1 it can be seen that, even in the operation of a small-scale program, a great number of potential and actual communication contexts exist in which program actors participate.

Observations and Interviews: Looking for Natural Questions and Answers

One of the differences between ethnography and other forms of research is that ethnographers do not automatically assume that they know the right questions to ask in a setting. In fact, as Spradley suggests, in ethnographic fieldwork "both questions and answers must be

	Patient	Staff	Sponsor	Management	Client	Researcher
Patient	Children interact in classroom	Play therapy sessions			Teacher and child interact in classroom	Researcher observes and interacts with children in classroom
Staff	Individual play therapy sessions	Supervision meetings once a week. Informal discussion (e.g., coffee, lunch, driving to and from DCC)	Meetings, informal discussions with agency director	Supervision meetings once per week. Informal mtgs, discussions, etc.	Report meetings two times per month with teachers at the day care center, informal discussions	Researcher attends supervision meetings and report meetings
Sponsor		Meetings, informal discussions with director		Supervisor meets with agency director, informal discussions		
Management		Supervision meetings once per week. Informal mtgs, coffee, lunch, driving	Supervisor meets with superiors		Program initiation meetings before program introduced. Report meetings	Researcher attends supervision meetings
Client	Child and teacher interact in classroom	"Report" meetings twice monthly, informal discussions		Supervisor meets with teachers in report meetings, and program initiation meetings	Teachers interact with each other in classroom, DCC staff meeting. Informal discussions, lunch, coffee, "nap time"	Researcher interacts formally and informally with teachers in classroom lunch, coffee, nap time, etc.
Researcher	Researcher observes and interacts with children in classroom	Researcher attends Supervision mtgs and report meetings		Researcher attends Supervision meetings	Researcher interacts formally and informally with teachers at DCC	

Figure 5.1. Communication Contexts for Program Actors: Eastside Day Care Center
NOTE: From "The Ethnographic Evaluation of Human Service Programs" by H. B. Schwartzman, 1983, *Anthropological Quarterly*, 56, p. 183, Figure 1. © Copyright 1983 by *Anthropological Quarterly*. Reprinted by permission.

discovered in the social situation being studied" (1979, p. 32). He cites Black and Metzger (1964):

It could be said of ethnography that until you know the question that someone in the culture is responding to you can't know many things about the responses. Yet the ethnographer is greeted, in the field, with an array of responses. He needs to know what questions people are answering in their every act. He needs to know which questions are being taken for granted because they are what "everybody knows" without thinking. . . . Thus the task of the ethnographer is to discover questions that seek the relationships among entities that are conceptually meaningful to the people under investigation. (p. 144)

Spradley argues that initially ethnographic data should be gathered by listening and observing, "not to discover answers but to find which questions to ask" (Spradley, 1970, p. 69). In Spradley and Mann's (1975) study of Brady's Bar, they found that one of the recurring questions waitresses ask is, "Who is the bartender tonight?" This was an important question because waitresses needed to have good relationships with bartenders in order to have their orders filled rapidly.

In *Number Our Days* (1978) Barbara Myerhoff utilized the expertise of Abe, the director of the Aliya Senior Citizens Center that she studied in Venice, California, to formulate what turned out to be important and productive questions for the Jewish elderly who were participating in Center activities:

Basha came out of the Center and Abe called to her, "Basha, how would you like to have the professor make a book from your life?" Basha did not hesitate. "You got a pencil? You want to get it down right. I begin with my childhood in Poland. Tell me if I go too fast. Naturally, it's a long story." (p. 35)

In one way or another Myerhoff found that the seniors were asking themselves questions like "What does it mean to be a Jew?" and "What does it mean to grow old?" In Center life, as she came to understand it, she found "an entire, though miniature, society, a Blakeian 'world in a grain of sand' the setting for an intricate and rich culture, made up of bits and pieces of people's common history" (p. 9). Myerhoff was fortunate in discovering the questions that were important to her informants at the Center, and the success of her study came, in part, from the fact that she built her research methodology on these questions. In this case she developed a "Living History" class for the seniors, which gave them an opportunity to use their natural tendency for storytelling to explore a variety of common themes and to try to make sense of their lives, their identity, and the enormous changes that they had experienced:

Hitting on a format that allowed for storytelling was a fortunate accident. When we began the session, there was no way I could have anticipated the significance of these exchanges. In time it became clear that storytelling was a passion among these people, absolutely central to their culture. (Myerhoff, 1978, p. 37)

In choosing a format for her ethnography, Myerhoff built part of her presentation around these *bobbe-myseh* (grandmother's tales) because they were so central and important to the elders she was studying.

My research at Midwest Community Mental Health Center (CMHC) may also be used to illustrate the importance of looking for natural questions and answers. When I arrived at the Center I was asking questions about how the Center developed and implemented a paraprofessional model of treatment for chronically ill mental patients, but participants were asking themselves questions about their own leadership and authority relationships. It took me quite some time to hear *their* questions and answers and yet they were apparent in some of our earliest observations (see first encounter field notes) and interviews. In the following segment of an interview with the president of the executive board, the concerns and questions about authority and leadership were quite apparent. The questions are "What kind of leadership structure *do* we have?" and "What kind of leadership structure *should* we have?"

Researcher: Could you describe what is happening at the center now?

Informant: Well, they've been having meetings, you know, on some of the suggested changes that Paul [the acting Executive Director] has come up with, which really more or less come from NIMH dictates too, and that is that the NIMH is saying that there has to be a clearer delegation of authority from the Executive Director to the various heads of the various departments and so forth. There was too much of a flow from—they used to say at the center that there was not only a flow from the top down, but there was a flow from the bottom up, that the paraprofessionals could go directly to the Executive Director with their problems, etc. Well, this is all good, but there was never an ability on the part of Fred [former Executive Director] to delegate authority. It would always be undermined by Paula or someone else. And Sharon Jones is going to be head of emergency services, she should have the right to make certain decisions in that area, and not to be contramanded by Paula or someone else when she does it. There was too much of that. And what that means is that the Executive Director isn't getting his work done, because he doesn't delegate anything to anybody. That was one of the obvious problems at the center, and we used to call people coordinators. Someone asked Kenneth Nolan from NIMH, when he said we should have assistant directors, and someone said, "Well, what's the difference whether you call them an assistant director or a coordinator?" And he said, "In my mind, there's a big difference. Coordinators just coordinate things. An assistant director makes decisions at his level, and that's what we need." And so a lot of the suggested reorganization things are being dictated to us by NIMH to solve problems that he feels weren't solved before with our other structure. They want a more streamlined chart of organization than we had before. We always found fault with that before. Fred would put a chart on the wall and there'd be so many dotted lines and dash lines and intercrossing lines, and there would always be an explanation why that had to be because the clinical director is supposed to have input to here and to here and to here, and it always would sound like a good case for it, but I think if you can't really draw an organizational chart without getting it all confused, then right there there's an indication that there's something wrong. You've got to be able to draw it in some way, and we never really were able to. And it would always change from week to week and people would move around, too. There was too much of that.

Ethnographic Interviews

The above interview also illustrates the importance of asking very open and sometimes ambiguous questions in the early stages of research. These kinds of questions give the informant an opportunity to answer in ways and with content that is important to him or her—not to the researcher. Spradley (1979, p. 86) refers to these as "descriptive" or "grand tour" questions and he suggests that they be focused on *what*, as opposed to *why*, questions. The purpose of these questions is to collect a large sample of the informant's speech and to elicit key terms/folk terms in the context of their use. Following this, "mini-tour questions may be used to ask more detailed questions about specific terms, activities or objects" (see Spradley, 1979, for further elaboration on these questioning techniques).

The ethnographic interviewer should avoid translating what an informant says into the researcher's own theories or terms, or telling the informant what he or she is feeling or experiencing, or interrupting an informant during his or her response to a question. The following interview, also from the Midwest study, illustrates what not to do when conducting ethnographic interviews in an organization:

Researcher: What happened in the training sessions?

Interviewee: In some ways it seems real complicated. There is a lot of history. I often walked away from encounters feeling out of my fucking mind. I was really in a double bind like if I said I wanted to understand or there were things that I didn't know about certain racial or ethic groups and economic strata Paula [clinical director] would say, "Yes, there are a lot of things you don't know, even as a professional you're really dumb, you need a lot of education or re-education." But, on the other hand if I said, "You know, I really haven't had contact with poor people, but I do understand some things about other groups, not a lot, I have not had that much contact, I have never been black and I have never been poor, but I am a person and I do have feelings and so these other people have feelings." They would say, "That's a typical liberal attitude," that because I care and I want to know, that automatically means I can't understand and I don't recognize that there is a terrible distance between us.

Researcher: In other words, if I follow you correctly, Paula accused you of psychological false consciousness, the more you profess sympathy and a willingness to learn, the more that was evidence that you were protecting your psychological class privileges. Is that kind of how she interpreted?

Interviewee: Yes.

Researcher: In other words, from the way you experienced it, it was kind of a no-win situation, whatever position you took was evidence that you really weren't about to change.

Interviewee: Not only not about to change, but I also wasn't really in touch with any real feelings, that I wasn't somehow giving her enough evidence that I was . . . (*interruption*)

As can be seen in this segment the researcher's tendency to translate, "lead the witness," and even interrupt the interviewee ultimately produced shortened responses to research questions. This is exactly the opposite of what the goal of an ethnographic interview is. Responses that build on terms, expressions, or experiences used by the informant are much more likely to produce richer informant responses to questions. For example, a more effective response to the informant's first statement in this interview would be: "That's really interesting and it seems really complicated, could you say some more about how you felt in a 'double bind' at the training sessions?"

Kathleen Gregory also discusses the importance of ethnographic interviews in her research with computer technical professionals in Silicon Valley. The focus of this research was on "native concepts for social categories and on identifying those with contrasting orientations or cultures" (1983, p. 366). This approach and the development of taxonomies displaying these differences and their significance have already been discussed in Chapter 3. In this research Gregory also illustrates the value or putting the informant in the expert (rather that the subject) role. In this case she used informant conceptions of representativeness to make decisions about which kinds of individuals to interview:

> Interviewees (both individual and corporate participants) were recruited according to native conceptions of representativeness, which emerged during successive interviews. Criteria they suggested included the type of company one worked for (e.g., large, stable development companies, start ups, research labs, software houses) amount of experience one had, seniority, sex, ethnicity, place and type of education, and, importantly, technical occupations or specialty. The participants identified a number of generic technical occupations, which were sampled, including software and engineering, hardware engineering, computer science, marketing technical writing or documentation, and technical management. (p. 366)

Drawing on more than 58 years of research on groups and organizations in American society and other countries, W. F. Whyte discusses interviewing strategy and tactics in *Learning from the Field* (1984). Here he specifically discusses the value of asking informants to comment on specific events when conducting field research interviews. In this case he is referring to a way to encourage informants in interviews to expand on their experiences using examples. "When the informant expresses an attitude apparently unconnected with any event already described, I say something like this: 'That's interesting. Have you had some experience that has led you to feel this way?' Almost invariably the informant will respond with an account of one or more relevant experiences" (1984, p. 102).

The importance of *accounts* of experiences, sometimes called *cases* (see Werner & Schoepfle, 1987), or *stories* in ethnographic research, has already been discussed in Chapter 3. Stories may appear naturally in the flow of an ethnographic interview or they may be encouraged by questions, such as suggested above by Whyte. At Midwest, individuals frequently used stories or cases to illustrate specific points and then proceeded to interpret these cases in the interview. For example, referring back to the interview with the president of the executive board, it can be seen that the informant moves back and forth between short examples of points and his interpretation of what these examples mean. He notes early in his response: "They used to say at the center that there was not only a flow from the top down, but there was a flow from the bottom up, that the paraprofessionals could go directly to the Executive Director with their problems, and so on." And then, with hardly a pause, he proceeds to interpret what this means: "Well, this is all good, but there was never an ability on the part of Fred [former Executive Director] to delegate authority. It would always be undermined by Paula or someone else." In order to illustrate how this process occurs in this particular interview, I reproduce the text below and boldface the story/cases and italicize the interpretations.

Researcher: Could you describe what is happening at the center now?

Informant: Well, they've been having meetings, you know, on some of the suggested changes that Peter [the acting Executive Director] has come up with, which really more or less come from NIMH dictates too, and that is that the NIMH is saying that there has to be a clearer delegation of authority from the executive director to the various heads of the various departments and so forth. There was too much of a flow from—**they used to say at the center that there was not only a flow from the top down, but there was a flow from the bottom up, that the paraprofessionals could go directly to the Executive Director with their problems.** *Well, this is all good, but there was never an ability on the part of Fred [former Executive Director] to delegate authority. It would always be undermined by Paula or someone else.* **And Sharon Jones is going to be head of emergency services, she should have the right to make certain decisions in that area, and not to be contramanded by Paula or someone else when she does it.** *There was too much of that. And what that means is that the executive director isn't getting his work done, because he doesn't delegate anything to anybody. That was one of the obvious problems, at the center,* **and we used to call people coordinators. Someone asked Kenneth Nolan from NIMH, when he said we should have assistant directors, and someone said, "Well, what's the difference whether you call them an assistant director or a coordinator?" And he said, "In my mind, there's a big difference. Coordinators just coordinate things. An assistant director makes decisions at his level, and that's what we need."** *And so a lot of the suggested reorganization things are being dictated to us by NIMH to solve problems that he feels weren't solved before with our other structure. They want a more streamlined chart of organization than we had before.* **We always found fault with that before. Fred would put a chart on the wall and there'd be**

so many dotted lines and dash lines and intercrossing lines, and there would always be an explanation why that had to be because the clinical director is supposed to have input to here and to here and to here, and it always would sound like a good case for it, *but I think if you can't really draw an organizational chart without getting it all confused, then right there there's an indication that there's something wrong. You've got to be able to draw it in some way, and we never really were able to.* And it would always change from week to week and people would move around, too. *There was too much of that.*

Stories are an important source of data for organizational ethnographers because they are often natural answers to the recurring questions that individuals in organizations ask themselves. Questions like: "What kind of organization is this?" "Who are heroes, heroines, and villains?" "What do our heroes say about us?" "How do we make decisions?" "Who really makes decisions?" The continual narration of organizational stories can shape and reshape the way that individuals experience their organization, as my research at Midwest suggests, but stories are not always easy to investigate.

I conducted research with my husband, John Schwartzman, in a food technology corporation between 1989 and 1990. Because this was proprietary research I cannot report the results here, but I can describe the method we used to elicit, examine, and analyze a corpus of stories from this organization. This project was explicitly focused on stories and storytelling in a corporate context and it was short-term (approximately 4 months, then later extended for 6 months). We used key informant interviewing, working first with individuals chosen by a management group, but by a process of recommendations and volunteers we were able to significantly expand our informant group. Ideally it would have been best to spend more time using participant observation in order to see how stories appeared in natural situations, but because of time constraints we collected most stories using open-ended ethnographic interviews of the type discussed above, which encouraged individuals to talk about a broad range of topics (e.g., what they were currently doing in the company, what their early experience of the company had been, their role in specific projects, and the like). Frequently in discussing these kinds of issues, individuals would use stories to describe something (e.g., "I remember one time when [story follows]"); and after conducting and analyzing interviews with more than 30 individuals from several different positions within the company, we were able to see patterns in the stories individuals used to illustrate points. Most interesting were the differences we noted in how individuals remembered both *their* history in the company and the company's history in general. These differences seemed to relate directly to how individuals interpreted what would happen to the company in the future. The stories were grouped in three ways, again according to the variety of stories that we heard: stories about events (especially historical events), stories about individuals, and stories that invoked or illustrated particular cultural values. (Some of the values were values that the company attempted to self-consciously produce, and some were values that seemed pervasive and yet were not explicitly mentioned as values or ideals of this particular company.) Depending on the individual picked, stories about individuals were also told in ways that illustrated particular values (e.g., what happened to x? why x was right/wrong, who the "real" heroes were and why).

It is important to emphasize here that we tried to avoid asking questions like "tell me a story." When we did use this technique we found that individuals did not provide story responses. However, when engaged in open-ended ethnographic interviews, our informants moved much more naturally to using examples or stories to illustrate the points they were making. When this did not happen, following Whyte's suggestions, we then asked informants to give us examples or illustrations of points and/or issues that they raised.

Analyzing Events and Routines

The importance of combining interviews about events with observations of events has already been discussed as this was developed by the Hawthorne and Yankee City researchers. This approach calls attention to the importance of examining the everyday routines and occasions that bring people together in specific organizational contexts. The value of studying everyday routines has also been discussed in Chapter 3. The context analysis grid discussed earlier is helpful in specifying the variety of participants and recurring events and routines that the structure of a program or organization can generate. In the ethnography of speaking and communication literature, the event or scene as "the point at which speakers and means come together in use" (Bauman & Sherzer, 1975, p. 109) has been central for analysis. Once events have been identified, the ethnography of communication literature is also useful for developing an approach for describing and analyzing the significant components of specific events and their functions in specific settings. To illustrate how this approach can be applied to the study of organizations, I use Hymes's (1974) model to examine the specific components of meetings as communication events.

Participants: Describe the participants who interact with one another in a meeting, as speaker or sender, hearer or receiver of messages, and the relationships and responsibilities of these individuals to each other and also, possibly, to outside "constituencies" are of interest here.

Channels and Codes: Examine the channels for communication that may exist in a setting, for example, speaking, writing, drumming, singing, computer messages, and so on. The codes that may or may not be shared by participants include linguistic, paralinguistic, kinesic, musical, as well as interactive codes. In Hymes' *Speaking* model, these components are referred to as "Instrumentalities."

Space and Time: Note the spatial arrangement for the meeting and the time when it occurs. The various ways that meetings are negotiated and times are fixed for formal meetings are also important to describe.

Frame: The process or processes whereby the beginning, and ending, as well as the continuation of the meeting as an event, are signaled or marked are important to note. As a frame the meeting also provides participants with an interpretive context, using culturally standardized meta-communicative processes, for evaluating the significance and meaning of the event, that is, "this is serious," "this is work."

Meeting Talk: A number of components and their relationship to each other may be considered here in an attempt to describe the nature of meeting talk.

Topic and Results—The specific issue, concern, task, focus of the meeting, or what the meeting is about from the participants' perspective, for example, to make a decision about the hiring of a new executive director, to decide on new marketing strategies for a particular product, to formulate economic policy. This component also includes attention to the kinds of results which participants expect from a meeting (e.g., the belief that a meeting *should* produce a decision or some other type of obvious action).

Norms of Speaking and Interaction—An important process in meetings is the development and maintenance of a central focus of discussion, as meetings may be characterized by the way they move between central and peripheral or side-issue discussions. Speech and interaction rules that seem to be particularly important here are turn-taking rules and processes, the presence or absence of a meeting "chair," and rules and regulations available or developed for regulating debate (e.g., *Robert's Rules of Order*). Included here is also the decision rule, if any, which a group uses (e.g., consensus or majority rule) and the expectation as to whether the "decision," "action" is binding on participants.

Oratorical Genres and Styles—Specific forms of speech, which may occur in other events (e.g., proverbs, jokes, prayers), may also be part of a meeting. In addition, specific speech-making styles may also be associated with particular types of meetings as well as individuals and communities, for example, the use of indirect or allusive speech in formal or scheduled meetings versus the use of direct speech in informal or unscheduled meetings.

Interest and Participation—The means, sanctions, and rewards that may be used to encourage or demand participation at meetings, as well as to maintain interest or involvement in an event in progress.

Norms of Interpretation: Examine the processes that participants have developed for interpreting what happens in meetings. This involves relating meetings to other speech events (e.g., chats and stories) that may become important for individuals to use to make sense of meetings.

Goals and Outcomes: Following Hymes (1974, p. 57) and also Duranti (1984, p. 222) it is useful to distinguish between the *goals* of specific individuals in a meeting, which may be various (e.g., to have their particular candidate hired, to block the hiring of someone else's candidate), and the *outcome* of the event from the standpoint of a community, organization, or culture. The interrelationship between these issues and especially the outcome of a meeting, as defined here, is discussed in more detail in Schwartzman (1989). Goals and outcomes, as defined and distinguished here, are also differentiated from topics and results, as discussed above.

Meeting Cycles and Patterns: The relationship of meetings to each other and to other types of communication events is also important to examine. These relationships are crucial for understanding the role that meetings play in the production and reproduction of social relations and cultural beliefs and values. These relationships are also important for understanding how meetings may either inhibit or facilitate the accomplishment of individual goals as well (adapted from Schwartzman, 1989, pp. 67-69).

When events such as meetings or sales talks or storytelling become a topic for research, then their existence becomes problematic and not everyday. This approach to the study of meetings as everyday organizational routines raises several questions for researchers. How, in fact, do individuals construct meetings as communicative events? What local knowledge do participants use to produce and recognize a meeting as a significant event? What are the types of meetings that individuals in particular settings recognize, and how do they interpret the significance of their meeting? How do meetings interact with other events, including other meetings, to reproduce themselves and the organization?

Hearing Voices and Representing Them: Experiments in Writing Organizational Ethnographies

> For me, the anthropological voice has fundamentally to do with the inclination to hear voices. An important part of our vocation is "listening to voices," and our methods are the procedures that best enable us to hear voices, to represent voices, to translate voices. Anthropological work that does not contain voices somehow misses its calling. It is work that misses our opportunity to listen to voices. If it does not contain that authentic voices of the subjects of investigation, throw it aside, because it does not have lasting value. Anthropology is a paying attention to the voices of those among whom we live and study. (Fernandez, 1987, p. 12)

The process of researching and writing an ethnography is characterized by several tensions. First there is the tension between trying to represent the native's point of view and then also trying to articulate what is taken for granted by one's informants (explicit and implicit culture). In the Hawthorne research this tension existed between the interviewer and the observer, who focused respectively on what people said and what people did. Second is the tension between representing the native's voice, as Fernandez suggests, and recognizing and finding some way to represent the anthropologist's voice—one of the concerns of recent experiments in writing ethnographies. Finally, there is the tension between representing local cultural worlds and their relationship to larger systems of political economy (Marcus & Fisher, 1986,

p. 77). In my view the goal of ethnography is not to resolve these tensions but to recognize and creatively exploit them.

The problems of representing the lives of "others" has recently become a focus for discussion and controversy in anthropology and the other social sciences (see Clifford, 1988; Clifford & Marcus, 1986; Marcus & Fisher, 1986; Van Maanen, 1988). A number of issues have been raised in this discussion, such as questions about how the authority of narrators is established, the possibility of incorporating multiple narrators into one's work, the importance of thinking about how knowledge and experience are portrayed in ethnographies, ways to include the voice of the ethnographer in the ethnography, and the political implications of representations. Ethnographers have tried to deal with several of these issues by experimenting with various ways and formats for representing the lives of those whom they study. Marcus and Fisher review a number of experimental ethnographies published in the 1970s and 1980s (e.g., Crapazano, 1980; Favret-Saada, 1980; Price, 1983). The urge to experiment with the form of ethnographies is now becoming apparent in the organizational literature as well.

DON'T SHOOT THE FIELDWORKER

Van Maanen illustrates the value of experimenting with what he calls "impressionist tales" in his book, *Tales of the Field* (1988). Using his fieldwork with police in Union City, he tells the story of an eventful night shift, which includes a car chase, car theft, and fear and bumbling on the part of the police and the ethnographer (pp. 109-119). In "One with a Gun, One with a Dog, and One with the Shivers," all of this comes together in an engaging tale that represents, in a way that conventional ethnographic writing does not, the feel of both police work and fieldwork, with all its thrills, frustrations, and confusions:

> I run toward the car to get the sturdy multicell flashlight, a copper's tool that gets more service as an effective truncheon than as a source of light. At the car, bumblebee policing—swarming—is in full glory. There are five patrol units plus the K-9 (canine) unit, whose driver arrives saying breathlessly, "not bad time, eh?"
>
> I point the men in the general direction of where I'd left David and scramble around in the car to find the flashlight. I find it under the front seat and run back up the driveway to find a half-dozen cops stomping through the bushes, all with guns drawn. I'm standing in civic garb, trembling, and thinking, "Don't shoot the fieldworker." (p. 112)

MYSTERY . . . IS A GOOD PLACE TO BEGIN FIELD RESEARCH

In *Casing a Promised Land* (1986), H. L. Goodall also experiments with the storytelling form (in this case the detective novel) as a way to present a series of ethnographies of organizations in the Huntsville, Alabama, area. In this way we learn about, among other things, the transition of the Huntsville office of a Boston-based computer company, the United States Army's Star Wars Command, the United States Space Academy's Space Camp, shopping malls, and professional meetings. The detective mystery and the detective role figure prominently in these depictions as Goodall (narrator/ethnographer/detective) puts himself in his "stories" that begin in mystery and end in at least a temporary resolution of it (p. xii).

In Goodall's terms, when organizations are approached as a mystery, "the answers are always in the reading" (p. 9). In his chapter, "Notes on a Cultural Evolution: The Remaking of a Software Company," he illustrates how company artifacts and space may be read as texts that carry important messages about an organizational setting. Operating in the detective role, he examines the meaning of symbols and seemingly unrelated artifacts and space at a Boston-based computer software company (B-BCSC). He begins, surprisingly, in the parking lot:

> You can learn to ask questions about the culture of an organization by examining the content of its parking lot. . . . The cars you pass in the B-BCSC parking lot are artifacts of the interchange of traffics public and private, and they . . . suggest realities whose appearances are of primary cultural importance. Honda, Chevrolet, Buick, Toyota, another Honda, another Honda, another Buick, a Fiat, a small Ford truck. . . . there are no motorcycles, bicycles, or multicolored Volkswagen microbuses.
>
> These are the cars and light trucks of aspiring, mostly boom-generation professionals who derive a way of knowing and being from the office that often follows them home. . . . Perhaps this is why a parking lot with only three red vehicles in it, and nothing vaguely exotic, not even a four-wheel drive, attracts attention, appeals to the sense of mystery that any cultural investigation begins with. There is much strategic ambiguity passing for beige and light blue and off white on cars that are uniformly protected by optional side moldings. They rest on either side of the B-BCSC building, straight rows of muted colors suggesting some sort of pattern. (1989, pp. 17-18)

After examining the parking lot, Goodall uses the narrative device of "the company tour" to move the reader into the symbolic system of B-BCSC (as he interprets it). We walk through the front door as he examines the company logo and the arrangement of the corridors, temporary walls, and colorful artifacts (posters, calendars, cartoons) that are displayed. Here he pays particular attention to contrasts between expected symbols (such as pictures of families, academic degrees) and unexpected expressions (such as "Shit Happens" stickers), which are "laced through the building next to degrees and family snapshots" (p. 27).

[THE SCIENTISTS] HAVE A LABORATORY
WE, ON THE OTHER HAND, HAVE A TEXT, THIS PRESENT TEXT

In order to examine the taken-for-granted assumptions of R. Guillemin's scientific research laboratory at the Salk Institute, Bruno Latour and Steve Woolgar portray this setting, as seen through the eyes of a fictional character, "the observer." The observer sees the laboratory as an unknown culture and at first he is confused and has a number of questions: "What are these people doing? What are they talking about? What is the purpose of these partitions or these walls? Why is this room in semidarkness whereas this bench is brightly lit? Why is everybody whispering? What part is played by the animals who squeak incessantly in anterooms?" (1986, p. 43).

But as the observer moves through the lab and starts to notice the multiple methods of "coding, marking, altering, correcting, reading and writing," this unfamiliar culture begins to look less confusing (p. 49):

At this point, the observer felt that the laboratory was by no means quite as confusing as he had first thought. It seemed that there might be an essential similarity between the inscription capabilities of apparatus, the manic passion for marking, coding, and filing, and the literary skills of writing, persuasion, and discussion. Thus, the observer could even make sense of such obscure activities as a technician grinding the brains of rats, by realizing that the eventual end product of such activity might be a highly valued diagram. Even the most complicated jumble of figures might eventually end up as part of some argument between "doctors." For the observer, then the laboratory began to take on the appearance of a system of literary inscription. (pp. 50-51)

70

In this study the research goal was to examine how the social order of a scientific laboratory was constructed, recognizing that there are always multiple readings of these processes and that scientists and researchers are engaged in the same process of order construction and literary inscription (p. 33). Eventually the observer and the ethnographers begin to see that what they are doing in their social science research and what the scientists are doing in their natural science investigations (neuroendocrinology) are very similar.

ETHNOGRAPHY AND ESTRANGEMENT

Dan Rose approaches the corporation in American society by examining the incorporation of life in America. This process is so familiar to us that it is sometimes difficult to recognize the way it influences our worldview and everyday practices, including our research:

One of the reasons that American culture remains enigmatic to us is that it has inherited on a massive scale the corporation as a colonizing form, that ethnographic practice grew up in this colonizing milieu and is one of its intellectual products, and that our ethnographic inquiry is conducted from within institutions. Ethnographers are rewarded by persons like themselves who spend most of their working lives inside relatively large nonprofit corporations such as the university and the scholarly association, to mention two. The social forms that cage our intellectual activities remain all too invisible to us. (1989, p. 12)

Anthropologists are well situated to examine and challenge the processes of organizational life and incorporation that have become so familiar to us that we do not seem to see them. To bring these processes to our attention, Rose explores the motifs of estrangement and incorporation in American society in *Patterns of American Culture* (1989). In a two-part experimental critique and fable, Rose examines "precapitalist forms of exchange" observed in his fieldwork among African-Americans in South Philadelphia, and the multiple ways that capitalist corporate forms shape and, in fact, saturate our existence. He uses lengthy examples of his own experiences with incorporation to illustrate his points. In "Masks," his ethnographic fable, he presents a view of life and death in a fictional society that is also a comment on the practice of ethnography.

YOU AND I HAVE SIMPLY GOT TO STOP MEETING THIS WAY

In my own work (Schwartzman, 1989) I chose to present my ethnography of life at Midwest as seen through the meetings that staff used to constitute and make sense of the organization. In telling this story, each of the chapters in the book places a meeting, or meetings, in the foreground for understanding the actions that are described, and presents a critique of concepts typically used in organizational and anthropological research for understanding events in the organization. In this way the giveness of history, environment, and ideology is questioned by "the council meeting" and "the training meeting." The unquestioned assumption of the importance of decisions in organizational systems, as well as materialist and individualistic definitions of power, are challenged by "the committee meeting" and "the board meeting," and the value of what are presumed to be *expressive* activities is questioned by "the staff meeting." Meetings have generally been the background structure for examining and assessing what are assumed to be the *really* important matters of organizational life, for example, power, decisions, ideology, and conflict. In this book these concepts become the background structures for examining the significance of specific meetings at the Center, and these meetings are used in turn to critique these standard concepts.

PERFORMING CULTURE

One of the most novel approaches that a few researchers have begun to use for the presentation of their ethnographies is to adopt the role of performer. A number of interesting projects in this area have been attempted by researchers at Northwestern University, sparked by the work of Dwight Conquergood and Howard Becker (themselves influenced by the work of Victor Turner, 1986, and Richard Schenecher, 1985). For example, Conquergood (1990) has just completed a film and performance on gang organization and culture (*The Heart Broken in Half*).[3] Two other recent works illustrate how researchers may work with actors or themselves perform texts, developed from ethnographic research, in a specific attempt to critique institutional structures and relationships. Mariane Paget (1990) uses this approach to examine physician/patient communication and miscommunication. An even more recent study by Wellin (1991) uses fieldwork in a group home for women diagnosed with Alzheimer's disease as the basis for a performance that attempts to illustrate "how the deterioration of identity among institutionalized elderly is determined by organizational and interactional, as well as organic, processes" (p. 2).

Summary

Ethnography is a cyclical process that provides researchers with a way to examine cultures from the inside out. In this chapter I discussed some of the major stages, as well as processes, of ethnography in organizations, from entry into a setting to recent experiments in writing organizational ethnographies. The tensions inherent in conducting ethnography were also examined, tensions between explicit and implicit culture (saying and doing), between the native's voice and the anthropologist's voice, and between representations of the local cultural world and larger worlds. These tensions appear in both past and present studies and, in my view, they are responsible, at least in part, for the creativity and serendipity associated with the ethnographic method. What is most interesting about recent trends in writing organizational ethnographies is that in these texts researchers are no longer worrying about or trying to hide, these tensions but instead they are recognizing and creatively exploiting them in their representations of organizational life.

NOTES

1. Steven Barnett is observing how individuals behave when they drive to suggest product and design changes for Nissan North America (*The New York Times*, 1991); Lorna McDougal is examining different approaches to improving staff training for Arthur Andersen (*The New York Times*, 1991); Lucy Suchman is working with Xerox Corporation's Palo Alto Research Center on a study of workplace design (*The New York Times*, 1991); Roger McConochie is examining cross-cultural factors in airline safety for Boeing Co. (*Chicago Tribune*, April 28, 1991); Rita Denny has recently worked with the Campbell Soup Company to understand relations between consumers and microwave ovens (*Crain's Chicago Business*, April 9, 1990); Madeline Tram worked with a large laundry service in New York City to examine problems of alcoholism and absenteeism at one of its branches (*The New York Times*, 1991); Elizabeth Briody is working for General Motors to investigate repatriation experiences for employees (see Briody & Baba, 1991) and to examine barriers to implementing computer systems (*The New York Times*, 1991).

2. In many ways ethnographers are like explorers (see Spradley, 1980, p. 26) and the significant thing about explorers, as Bateson (1972) has suggested, is that you cannot know what you are exploring until you have explored it.

3. Information on Dwight Conquergood's film, *The Heart Broken in Half*, may be obtained by contacting the Department of Performance Studies, Theatre & Interpretation Building, 1979 Sheridan Road, Northwestern University, Evanston, IL, 60208 (708) 491-3171.

6. CONCLUSION

I'm the last guy here because last Friday, the 19th of June, the last AT&T fellows left. There were about five of them, one supervisor and a handful of mechanics and they finished all of their things that they had to do with regard to the property sale, they had to finish up some environmental clean-up and get rid of some hazardous materials and they were done. So I feel real naked now. Here comes Monday morning, I don't have anybody to help me out if something goes wrong in the power plant. I got to depend on my own judgment and so on. I've got almost half way through the week and things are still going alright. Now we're on our own. I guess maybe the best way for me to describe my relations with AT&T—AT&T is really a foreign word—I'm a Western Electric employee.

Tom, the last Western Electric
employee at the Hawthorne plant,
June 24, 1987

In organizing this book I chose to focus attention on the Hawthorne study because of its prominence as the first, and also most controversial, social science study of a modern American complex organization and because of the role anthropologists played in suggesting methods and models for the design of the project. As illustrated in this book, the effect of the Hawthorne study has been far-reaching, although not always in ways that researchers have realized. Burrell and Morgan (1979) argue that the Hawthorne study is significant because of its theoretical influence, especially the introduction of systems equilibrium concepts and an organic metaphor (as taken from the work of Durkheim, Malinowski, Pareto, and Radcliffe-Brown) into the organizational literature. While agreeing with their argument I suggest that the study is also important because of what it tells us about the value of using *ethnography in organizations*. Since this is a book about ethnography in organizations it seemed important to highlight the project that initiated the use of this method in organizational research.

The question of "what *really* happened at Hawthorne?" continues to trouble researchers and motivate continued scrutiny and criticism of the Hawthorne studies (see Richard Gillespie's most recent analysis of conflict and dissent within the Hawthorne research group itself, *Manufacturing Knowledge*, 1991). In my view the Hawthorne research is most interesting because it foreshadowed many of the changes and clashes in theoretical and methodological orientation that have been played out

Figure 6.1. Sunday, April 12, 1987, "Building 27" Hawthorne Works Demolished. Photo by Randy Lee Belice. Reprinted by permission of the *Chicago Sun-Times*.

Figure 6.2. Hawthorne Works Shopping Center

over the years in the organizational field. In this book I have tried to examine some of these changes and clashes specifically as they have influenced the development of an anthropological/ethnographic orientation to the study of organizations. The one organization that has been neglected in all of the debates, controversies, and analyses that continue to surround the Hawthorne study is the Hawthorne plant itself. For researchers it is still 1927 and "the girls" in the Relay Assembly Test Room are still assembling small electrical relays for telephones, frozen in time by research representations and controversies. Of course it is not 1927, and the girls are no longer working, and so I conclude this book with a postscript on "what happened to Hawthorne."

Postscript: In 1986 AT&T Technologies sold the land and buildings of the Hawthorne Works to the Hawthorne Partners, a group of commercial real estate developers, who converted this facility into a shopping center and location for warehousing and light manufacturing.[1] In April 1987 the building that had housed the Hawthorne Studies Room at the plant was demolished to make way for a shopping center, which was opened in 1988.[2] No longer the site for the assembly of telephones or the manufacture of pulp cable, copper rod, wire, relays, and capacitors, the Hawthorne Works shopping center is now the location for Handy Andy, an Omni Super Store, Fashion Bug, Rent a Center, Giant Auto Supply, St. Paul Federal Bank, Taco Bell, and many other stores. And so the story of the Hawthorne plant itself, transformed from a large-scale industrial complex to a mixed-use redevelopment project, continues to unfold and reflect the multitude of changes that have occurred in the United States urban and organizational landscape.

NOTES

1. In 1990 the Hawthorne Partners sold the manufacturing and warehousing space to the Los Angeles-based Angeles Corporation, a diversified financial services firm.

2. The original Hawthorne studies records are now at Harvard University. Displays originally housed in the Hawthorne Studies Room at the Hawthorne plant are now at the AT&T Archives in Warren, New Jersey. In 1978 a museum to commemorate the factory's 75th anniversary was built, based on donations from employees, retired and active, and the Illinois Bell Telephone Company. This museum has now been donated to the Historical Society of Cicero and is currently housed in facilities at Morton High School in Cicero, Illinois.

REFERENCES

Andrews, J.A.Y., & Hirsch, P. M. (1983). Ambushes, shootouts and knights of the roundtable: The language of corporate takeovers. In L. R. Pondy, P. Frost, G. Morgan, & T. Dandridge (Eds.), *Organizational symbolism*. Greenwich, CT: JAI.

Applebaum, H. A. (1981). *Royal blue: The culture of construction workers*. New York: Holt, Rinehart & Winston.

Arensberg, C. (1951). Behavior and organization: Industrial studies. In J. Rohrer & M. Sherif (Eds.), *Social psychology at the crossroads*. New York: Harper & Row.

Arensberg, C., Barkin, S., Chalmers, W. E., Wilensky, H. L., Worthy, J. C., & Dennis, B. D. (Eds.). (1957). *Research in industrial human relations*. New York: Harper & Row.

77

Arensberg, C., & Kimball, S. (1965). *Culture and community*. New York: Harcourt Brace and World.

Baba, M. (1989). Organizational culture: Revisiting the small-society metaphor. *The Anthropology of Work Review* [Special Issue: Anthropological approaches to organizational culture, P. Sachs, Ed.]. Washington, DC: Society for the Anthropology of Work.

Bateson, G. (1972). *Steps to an ecology of mind*. New York: Ballantine.

Bauman, R., & Sherzer, J. (1975). The ethnography of speaking. *Annual Review of Anthropology, 4*, 95-119.

Black, M., & Metzger, D. (1964). Ethnographic description and the study of law. *American Anthropologist, 67*, 141-165.

Blau, P. M. (1963). *The dynamics of bureaucracy* (rev. ed.). Chicago: University of Chicago Press.

Boje, D. M., Fedor, D. B., & Rowland, K. M. (1982). Myth making: A qualitative step in interventions. *Journal of Applied Behavioral Science, 18*, 17-28.

Bourdieu, P. (1977). *Outline of a theory of practice*. Cambridge, UK: Cambridge University Press.

Bramel, D., & Friend, R. (1981). Hawthorne, the myth of the docile worker and class bias in psychology. *American Psychologist, 36*, 867-878.

Briody, E. K., & Baba, M. L. (1991). Explaining differences in repatriation experiences: The discovery of coupled and decoupled systems. *American Anthropologist, 93*, 322-344.

Britan, G., & Cohen, R. (Eds.). (1980). *Hierarchy and society: Anthropological perspectives on bureaucracy*. Philadelphia: ISHI Press.

Burawoy, M. (1979). The anthropology of industrial work. *Annual Review of Anthropology, 8*, 231-266.

Burrell, G., & Morgan, G. (1979). *Sociological paradigms and organizational analysis*. London: Heineman.

Carey, A. (1967). The Hawthorne studies: A radical criticism. *American Sociological Review, 32*, 403-416.

Caudill, W. (1958). *The psychiatric hospital as a small society*. Cambridge, MA: Harvard University Press.

Chapple, E. D. (1941). Organization problems in industry. *Applied Anthropology, 1*, 2-9.

Chapple, E. D. (1949a). Field methods and techniques. *Human Organization, 8*, 22-28.

Chapple, E. D. (1949b). The interaction chronograph: Its evolution and present application. *Personnel, 25*, 285-307.

Chapple, E. D. (1953). Applied anthropology in industry. In A. S. Kroeber (Ed.), *Anthropology today* (pp. 819-831). Chicago: University of Chicago Press.

Chapple, E. D., & Coon, C. (1942). *Principles of anthropology*. New York: Henry Holt.

Clark, B. R. (1972). The organizational saga in higher education. *Administrative Science Quarterly, 17*, 178-184.

Clegg, S., & Dunkerly, D. (1980). *Organization, class and control*. London: Routledge & Kegan Paul.

Clifford, J. (1988). *The predicament of culture*. Cambridge, MA: Harvard University Press.

Clifford, J., & Marcus, G. E. (1986). *Writing culture*. Berkeley: University of California Press.

Crapazano, V. (1980). *Tuhami: Portrait of a Moroccan*. Chicago: University of Chicago Press.

78

Dalton, M. (1959). *Men who manage*. New York: John Wiley.

Deal, T. E., & Kennedy, A. A. (1982). *Corporate cultures*. Reading, MA: Addison Wesley.

Devereux, G. (1949). The social structure of the hospital as a factor in total therapy. *American Journal of Orthopsychiatry, 19*, 492-500.

Dickson, W. J., & Roethlisberger, F. J. (1966). *Counseling in an organization: A sequel to the Hawthorne researches*. Cambridge, MA: Harvard University Press.

Drucker, P. (1974). *Management*. New York: Harper & Row.

Dubinskas, F. (Ed.). (1988). *Making time: Ethnographies of high-technology organizations*. Philadelphia: Temple University Press.

Dunsing, R. J. (1978). *You and I have simply got to stop meeting this way*. New York: AMACO.

Duranti, A. (1984). Lauga and Talanoago: Two speech genres in a Samoan political event. In D. L. Brenneis & F. R. Myers (Eds.), *Dangerous words: Language and politics in the Pacific* (pp. 217-242). New York; New York University Press. [Reissued 1991. Prospect Heights, IL: Waveland Press]

Eddy, E., & Partridge, W. L. (Eds.). (1978) *Applied anthropology in America*. New York: Columbia University Press.

Favret-Saada, J. (1980). *Deadly words: Witchcraft in the Bocage*. Cambridge, UK: Cambridge University Press.

Fernandez, J. (1987). Anthropology as a vocation: Listening to voices [Guest editorial]. In E. A. Schultz & R. H. Lavenda, *Cultural anthropology* (pp. 12-13). New York: West.

Finlay, W. (1991). [Review of *Manufacturing knowledge*]. *Science, 254*, 1820-1821.

Franke, R. H. & Kaul, J. D. (1978). The Hawthorne experiments: First statistical interpretation. *American Sociological Review, 43*, 623-643.

Gamst, F. C. (1977). An integrating view of the underlying premises of an industrial ethnology in the United States and Canada. *Anthropological Quarterly, 50*, 1-8.

Gamst, F. C. (1980). *The hoghead: An industrial ethnology of the locomotive engineer*. New York: Holt, Rinehart & Winston.

Gamst, F. C. (1981). Considerations for an anthropology of work. *Anthropology of Work Newsletter, 2*, 7-9.

Gardner, B., & Moore, D. G. (1964). *Human relations in industry*. Chicago: Irwin.

Giddens, A. (1984). *The constitution of society*. Berkeley: University of California Press.

Gillespie, R. (1991). *Manufacturing knowledge: A history of the Hawthorne experiments*. New York: Cambridge University Press.

Goodall, H. L. (1989). *Casing a promised land*. Carbondale: Southern Illinois University Press.

Gouldner, A. W. (1954a). *Patterns of industrial bureaucracy*. Glencoe, IL: Free Press.

Gouldner, A. W. (1954b). *Wildcat strike*. New York: Antioch.

Gregory, K. (1983). Native-view paradigms: Multiple cultures and culture conflicts in organizations. *Administrative Science Quarterly, 28*, 359-376.

Gregory, K. (1984). "Signing up": The culture and careers of Silicon Valley computer people. Doctoral dissertation, Department of Anthropology, Northwestern University, Evanston, IL.

Haire, M. (1957). Interpersonal relations in collective bargaining. In C. Arensberg, S. Barkin, W. E. Chalmers, H. L. Wilensky, J. C. Worthy, & B. D. Dennis (Eds.), *Research in industrial human relations* (pp. 182-191). New York: Harper & Row.

Handelman, D. (1978). Introduction: A recognition of bureaucracy. In D. Handelman & E. Leyton (Eds.), *Bureaucracy and world view* (pp. 1-14). Newfoundland: Memorial University of Newfoundland.

Hymes, D. (1974). *Foundations in sociolinguistics.* Philadelphia: University of Pennsylvania Press.

Jelinek, M., Smircich, L., & Hirsch, P. (1983). Introduction: A code of many colors. *Administrative Science Quarterly, 28,* 331-333.

Landsberger, H. A. (1958). *Hawthorne revisited.* Ithaca, NY: Cornell University Press.

Latour, B., & Woolgar, S. (1986). *Laboratory life: The construction of scientific facts.* Princeton, NJ: Princeton University Press.

Malinowski, B. (1922). *Argonauts of the western Pacific.* London: Routledge.

Malinowski, B. (1927). The problem of meaning in primitive languages. In C. K. Ogden & I. A. Richards (Eds.), *The meaning of meaning* [Supp. I, pp. 296-336]. New York: Harcourt, Brace.

March, J. G., & Olsen, J. P. (Eds.). (1976). *Ambiguity and choice in organizations.* Bergen, Norway: Universitetsforlaget.

Marcus, G., & Fischer, M. J. (1986). *Anthropology as cultural critique.* Chicago: University of Chicago Press.

Martin, J., Feldman, M. S., Hatch, M. J., & Sitkin, S. B. (1983). The uniqueness paradox in organizational stories. *Administrative Sciences Quarterly, 28*(32), 438-453.

Mattingly, C. F. (1989). *Thinking with stories: Story and experience in a clinical practice.* Doctoral dissertation, Department of Urban Studies and Planning and Anthropology/Archaeology Program, Massachusetts Institute of Technology.

Mattingly, C. F. (1991). Narrative reflections on practical action. In D. Schon (Ed.), *The reflective turn: Case studies in and on practice.* New York: Teachers College Press.

Mayo, E. (1949). *The social problems of an industrial civilisation.* London: Routledge & Kegan Paul.

McDermott, R. P., & Roth, D. R. (1978). The social organization of behavior: Interactional approaches. *Annual Review of Anthropology, 7,* 321-345.

Merton, R. K. (1968). *Social theory and social structure.* New York: Free Press.

Myerhoff, B. (1978). *Number our days.* New York: Simon & Schuster.

Myers, F. R. (1986). Reflections on a meeting: Structure, language and the polity in a small-scale society. *American Ethnologist, 13,* 430-447.

Nader, L. (1969). Up the anthropologist—Perspectives gained from studying up. In D. Hymes (Ed.), *Reinventing anthropology.* New York: Random House.

Nash, J. C. (1979). The anthropology of the multinational corporation. In G. Huizer & B. Mannheim (Eds.), *The politics of anthropology: From colonialism and sexism toward a view from below* (pp. 421-446). Paris: Mouton.

Nash, J. C. (1981a). The anthropology of work. *Anthropology of Work Newsletter, 2,* 3-7.

Nash, J. C. (1981b). Ethnographic aspects of the world capitalistic system. *Annual Review of Anthropology, 10,* 393-423.

Nash, J. C. (1989). *From tank town to high tech: The clash of community and industrial cycles.* Albany: State University of New York Press.

Newman, K. (1988). *Falling from grace: The meaning of downward mobility in American culture.* New York: Free Press.

Ogbu, J. U. (1981). School ethnography: A multilevel approach. *Anthropology and Education Quarterly, 14,* 3-29.

Ortner, S. (1984). Theory in anthropology since the sixties. *Comparative Studies in Society and History, 26*, 126-166.

Ouchi, W. G. (1981). *Theory Z.* Reading, MA: Addison-Wesley.

Pacanowsky, M. E., & O'Donnell-Trujillo, N. (1982). Communication and organizational culture. *Western Journal of Speech Communication, 46*, 115-130.

Paget, M. A. (1990) Performing the text. *Journal of Contemporary Ethnography, 19*, 136-155.

Parsons, H. M. (1974). What happened at Hawthorne? *Science, 183*, 922-932.

Peters, T. J., & Waterman, R. H. (1982). *In search of excellence.* New York: Warner.

Pilcher, W. W. (1972). *The Portland longshoremen.* New York: Holt, Rinehart & Winston.

Pitt-Rivers, A.L.F. (1927) *The clash of culture and the contact of races.* London: Routledge.

Price, R. (1983). *First-time: The historical vision of an Afro-American people.* Baltimore: The Johns Hopkins University Press.

Radcliffe-Brown, A. R. (1933). *The Andaman islanders.* Cambridge, UK: Cambridge University Press.

Radcliffe-Brown, A. R. (1952). *Structure and function in primitive society.* London: Cohen and West.

Ranson, S., Hinings, B., & Greenwood, R. (1980). The structuring of organizational structures. *Administrative Science Quarterly, 25, 1-17.*

Richardson, F.L.W., & Walker, C. (1948). *Human relations in an expanding company: A study of the manufacturing departments in the Endicott plant of the International Business Machines Corporation.* New Haven, CT: Yale University Management Center.

Roberts, K. H. (1970). On looking at an elephant: An evaluation of cross-cultural research related to organizations. In T. D. Weinshall (Ed.), *Culture and management* (pp. 56-104). Harmondsworth, UK: Penguin.

Roethlisberger, F. J., & Dickson, W. J. (1934). *Management and the worker: Technical vs. social organization in an industrial plant* [Division of Research, Business Research Studies No. 9]. Cambridge, MA: Harvard University, Graduate School of Business Administration.

Roethlisberger, F. J., & Dickson, W. J. (1939). *Management and the worker.* Cambridge, MA: Harvard University Press.

Rose, D. (1989). *Patterns of American culture.* Philadelphia: University of Pennsylvania Press.

Rose, J. (1975). *Industrial behavior: Theoretical developments since Taylor.* Harmondsworth, UK: Allen Lane.

Roy, D. (1952). Quota restrictions and goldbricking in a machine shop. *American Journal of Sociology, 57*, 427-442.

Roy, D. (1953). Work satisfaction and social reward in quota achievement: An analysis of piecework incentive. *American Sociological Review, 18*, 507-514.

Roy, D. (1954). Efficiency and the fix: Informal intergroup relations in a piece-work machine shop. *American Journal of Sociology, 60*, 255-266.

Roy, D. (1959). Banana time: Job satisfaction and informal interaction. *Human Organization, 18*, 158-168.

Sachs, P. (Ed.). (1989). [Special issue: Anthropological approaches to organizational culture]. *Anthropology of Work Review.* Washington, DC: Society for the Anthropology of Work.

Safa, H. (1986). Runaway shops and female employment: The search for cheap labor. In E. Leacock & H. Safa (Eds.), *Women's work* (pp. 58-71). South Hadley, MA: Bergin and Garvey.

Salisbury, R. (1962). *Structures of custodial care: An anthropological study of a state mental hospital.* Berkeley: University of California Press.

Sayles, L. (1957). Work group behavior and the larger organization. In C. Arensberg, S. Barkin, W. E. Chalmers, H. L. Wilensky, J. C. Worthy, & B. D. Dennis (Eds.), *Research in industrial human relations* (pp. 131-145). New York: Harper & Row.

Schenecher, R. (1985). *Between theater and anthropology.* Philadelphia: University of Philadelphia Press.

Schwartzman, H. B. (1980). The bureaucratic context of a community mental health center: The view from "up." In G. M. Britan & R. Cohen, (Eds.), *Hierarchy and society: Anthropological perspectives on bureaucracy* (pp. 45-59). Philadelphia, ISHI Press.

Schwartzman, H. B. (1983). The ethnographic evaluation of human service programs. *Anthropological Quarterly, 56,* 179-189.

Schwartzman, H. B. (1984). Stories at work: Play in an organizational context. In E. M. Bruner (Ed.), *Text, play, and story: The construction and reconstruction of self and society* (pp. 80-93). Washington, DC: American Ethnological Society [Reissued 1988. Prospect Heights, IL: Waveland Press].

Schwartzman, H. B. (1989). *The meeting: Gatherings in organizations and communities.* New York: Plenum.

Selznick, P. (1966). *TVA and the grass roots.* New York: Harper & Row.

Sibley, W. (1986, May). *Studying corporate culture.* Session organized for the Annual Meeting of the American Association for the Advancement of Science, Philadelphia.

Silverman, D. (1970). *The theory of organizations.* New York: Basic Books.

Siwalop, S. (1986). What's an anthropologist doing in my office? In A. Podolefsky & P. J. Brown (Eds.), *Applying anthropology* (pp. 171-172). Mountain View, CA: Mayfield.

Smircich, L. (1983). Concepts of culture and organizational analysis. *Administrative Science Quarterly, 28,* 339-358.

Spradley, J. (1970). *You owe yourself a drunk.* Boston: Little, Brown.

Spradley, J. (1979). *The ethnographic interview.* New York: Holt, Rinehart & Winston.

Spradley, J. (1980). *Participant observation.* New York: Holt, Rinehart & Winston.

Spradley, J. P., & Mann, B. (1975). *The cocktail waitress: Women's work in a man's place.* New York: John Wiley.

Taylor, F. W. (1947). *Scientific management.* New York: Harper & Row.

Tommerup, P. (1988). From trickster to father figure: Learning from mythologization of top management. In M. O. Jones, M. D. Moore, & R. C. Snyder, (Eds.), *Inside organizations* (pp. 319-331). Newbury Park, CA: Sage.

Trist, E. L., & Bamforth, K. W. (1951). Some social and psychological consequences of the Longwall method of coal-getting. *Human Relations, 4*(1), 3-38.

Turner, V. (1986). *The anthropology of performance.* New York: PAJ Publications.

Van Maanen, J. (1973). Observations on the making of policemen. *Human Organization, 32,* 407-418.

Van Maanen, J. (1977). Experiencing organizations. In J. Van Maanen (Ed.), *Organizational careers: Some new perspectives* (pp. 15-45). New York: John Wiley.

Van Maanen, J. (Ed.). (1979). [Special issue on qualitative methodology]. *Administrative Science Quarterly, 24.*

Van Maanen, J. (1982). Fieldwork on the beat. In J. Van Maanen, J. Dabbs, & R. Faulkner (Eds.), *Varieties of qualitative research* (pp. 103-151). Beverly Hills, CA: Sage.

Van Maanen, J. (1988). *Tales of the field.* Chicago: University of Chicago Press.

Walker, C. R., & Guest, R. A. (1952). *The man on the assembly line.* Cambridge, MA: Harvard University Press.

Wallerstein, I. (1974). *The modern world-system: Capitalist agriculture and the origins of the European world-economy in the sixteenth century.* New York: Academic Press.

Wallman, S. (Ed.). (1979). *Social anthropology of work* [ASA Monograph 19]. London: Academic Press.

Warner, W. L., & Low, J. L. (1947). *The social system of the modern factory.* New Haven, CT: Yale University Press.

Warner, W. L., & Lunt, P. S. (1941). *The social life of a modern community.* New Haven, CT: Yale University Press.

Weick, Karl E. (1979). *The social psychology of organizing* (2nd ed.). Reading, MA: Addison-Wesley.

Weinshall, T. D. (1970). *Culture and management.* Harmondsworth, UK: Penguin.

Wellin, C. (1991). *Life at Lake Home.* Performance Process Paper for Performance and Social Science. Northwestern University, Evanston, IL.

Werner, O., & Schoepfle, G. M. (1987). *Systematic fieldwork: Foundations of ethnography and interviewing.* Beverly Hills, CA: Sage.

Whyte, W. F. (1948). *Human relations in the restaurant industry.* New York: McGraw-Hill.

Whyte, W. F. (1969). *Organizational behavior: Theory and application.* Homewood, IL: Irwin-Dorsey.

Whyte, W. F. (1978). [Review of *The elusive phenomena*]. *Human Organization, 37,* 412-420.

Whyte, W. F. (1984). *Learning from the field.* Beverly Hills, CA: Sage.

Wilensky, H. L. (1957). Human relations in the workplace: An appraisal of some recent research. In C. Arensberg, S. Barkin, W. E. Chalmers, H. L. Wilensky, J. C. Worthy, & B. D. Dennis (Eds.), *Research in industrial human relations* (pp. 25-50). New York: Harper & Row.

Wolfe, A. W. (1977).The supranational organization of production: An evolutionary perspective. *Current Anthropology, 19,* 615-635.

ABOUT THE AUTHOR

HELEN B. SCHWARTZMAN is a Professor in the Department of Anthropology at Northwestern University. She began her research as a student of children's play in a day-care center in a Chicago neighborhood. Over the years she has conducted research in a variety of organizational settings, including a community mental health center in a "psychiatric ghetto," mental health treatment facilities for children and adolescents in the state of Illinois, a highly profitable food technology company in the Chicago suburbs, and the transformation of the Western Electric Hawthorne Plant into a shopping center site. Dr. Schwartzman is the author of numerous articles on the topics of play, work, and organizations in American society and she is also the author of three books, *Transformations: The Anthropology of Children's Play, Play and Culture* (edited), and *The Meeting: Gatherings in Organizations and Communities*.